Ralf Nestmeyer

111 Places
in Provence
That You Must
Not Miss

emons:

Bibliographical information of the Deutsche Nationalbibliothek
The Deutsche Nationalbibliothek lists this publication
in the Deutsche Nationalbibliografie; detailed bibliographical
data are available on the internet at http://dnb.d-nb.de.

© Emons Verlag GmbH
All rights reserved
© All photographs: Ralf Nestmeyer, except p. 123, Circuit Paul Ricard, ERDA
Design: Eva Kraskes, based on a conception
by Lübbeke | Naumann | Thoben
Maps: altancicek.design, www.altancicek.de
Forest and built-up areas: Openstreetmap
English translation: John Sykes
Printing and binding: Grafisches Centrum Cuno, Calbe
Printed in Germany 2014
ISBN 978-3-95451-422-9
First edition

Did you enjoy it? Do you want more?
Join us in uncovering new places around the world on:
www.111places.com

Foreword

The name of Provence alone brings to mind associations and dreams of village squares shaded by plane trees, the Mediterranean life, the scent of lavender, thyme, rosemary and wild garlic. Yet beyond the fields of lavender and the olive groves, Provence has a huge variety of scenery that is not always sufficiently appreciated in travel literature. The Marais du Vigueirat, for example, a paradise for birds; the heavenly sandy beaches of the Camargue directly adjoining the industrial area of Fos-sur-Mer; and the Étang de Berre, a brackish lake with an extremely fragile ecosystem.

In terms of cultural history, too, Provence has much more to offer than the Papal Palace and the Pont du Gard. Not many people know about the historic quays of La Ciotat and the unique flood wall that encircles Caderousse. Very few travellers are aware that significant exiled artists such as Lion Feuchtwanger were once interned in the brickworks of Les Milles or that Le Corbusier designed a "living machine" in Marseille that looks like a stranded ocean liner. Another little-known fact is that one of the largest and most attractive bookshops in France is located in a remote village in Haute-Provence. And how many visitors know where in Provence to buy metre-long salamis, or that the world's deepest karst spring is to be found here?

This book takes you to 111 places in Provence whose special charm or unusual characteristics are a source of delight. From a crocodile farm to natural refrigerators, from deserted villages to remote mountain peaks, off the beaten track there are many big and small surprises that even the locals do not know about.

111 Places

1   The Brickworks of Les Milles

An almost forgotten internment camp

When we think of Provence, we think of fields of lavender and cicadas, savoir-vivre and Mediterranean light-heartedness, not of the suffering and horror of the Nazi period. Nevertheless, it is only a few kilometres from the brightness of Aix-en-Provence to the brickworks of Les Milles, where at times up to 3000 people were interned behind barbed wire between 1939 and 1943.

At the end of Les Milles there still stands a spacious complex of several warehouses that played an infamous part in Franco-German history. The writers, journalists, scientists, painters, musicians, politicians and actors who were imprisoned here during those years included such notable figures as the novelist Lion Feuchtwanger, the artist Max Ernst, the historian Golo Mann and the writers Alfred Kantorowicz and Walter Hasenclever. While Hasenclever, fearing deportation, took his own life on 21 June 1940 with an overdose of Veronal, Feuchtwanger and Kantorowicz gave literary expression to their experiences. Lion Feuchtwanger aimed criticism at the administration of the Vichy regime in The Devil in France, and Kantorowicz took up a clear position in Exile in France, both of them castigating the inhuman hygienic and psychological conditions in the camp.

It was a long time before attention was paid to this chapter of the past, which was commemorated in the summer of 2012 with a fitting monument in the form of the Mémorial National des Milles. At the center of this memorial is the room in which the guards once ate. Here a fine cycle of paintings was discovered in the 1970s, undoubtedly the work of German artists who were interned in Les Milles. The anonymous pictures entitled "Land of Plenty," "Grape Picking" and "Harvest," painted directly onto the concrete walls, tell of the privations of imprisonment, and dreams of peace and freedom.

Address 40, Chemin de la Badesse, 13547 Aix-en-Provence, www.campdesmilles.org | Directions Les Milles is on the D9, five kilometres southeast of Aix-en-Provence. The brickworks is in the west of Les Milles near the cemetery. | Opening times Tue–Sun 10am–6pm | Tip Opposite the brickworks is a historic rail truck in which the Jews who were held in Les Milles were deported to Auschwitz. Only 172 out of the more than 2000 people who were deported survived.

2__The Monument Joseph Sec

A mysterious monument to revolution

The dreamy squares and fountains of Aix-en-Provence, along with the Cathedral and Musée Granet, are part of the standard itinerary for a trip to this elegant city. But in the Monument Joseph Sec there is a mysterious sight that no guidebook describes, even though it is among the few examples of architecture from the time of the Revolution in all of France.

Admittedly, the mausoleum known as Monument Joseph Sec is easy to overlook, as it lies hidden in the garden of the health department of Aix and is only accessible during the office's open hours. Joseph Sec (1715–94) was a wealthy timber dealer from Aix-en-Provence, and wished to create a monument to himself by means of this mausoleum. About ten years before his death – before the French Revolution, that is – work commenced.

As a legacy that speaks to posterity, this prestigious monument stands for the values that its initiator represented with passion and pathos all his life: Joseph Sec was not only a devout Catholic but a member of the Grey Penitents ("Pénitents gris"), who did a great deal for charity. As a consequence of his deeply bourgeois attitudes he was also a committed Jacobin and supporter of Robespierre. Therefore the reliefs quote scenes from the Bible, especially from the New Testament, but are also influenced by the symbolism of Freemasonry and the French Revolution. Joseph Sec was devoted to the principles of the Enlightenment with an almost religious fervour. It is no coincidence that the statue representing revolutionary justice stands above one of Moses that took its inspiration from Michelangelo. The inscriptions, too, make this clear: "Having escaped from cruel slavery, henceforth I am my own master alone, yet I shall not use this freedom, because I owe obedience to the law."

Address 6, Avenue Pasteur, 13100 Aix-en-Provence | Directions Aix-en-Provence is at the intersection of the A 8 and A 51. Avenue Pasteur lies on the northern edge of the historic quarter. | Opening times Mon–Fri 8am–4pm | Tip It is only ten minutes' walk to the Pavillon de Vendôme, a 17th-century aristocratic mansion (Rue de la Molle).

3__ The Oppidum
Stormed by the Romans

Very few visitors to Aix-en-Provence follow the signs that lead upwards to the Oppidum d'Entremont. While the bustle on Cours Mirabeau and in front of Cézanne's studio is as lively as in the summer sales, a positively monastic tranquillity characterises the strong defensive walls of the Oppidum. You can stroll alone through the foundations of a Celto-Ligurian town whose fate is closely linked to that of Provence.

Entremont – the Celtic name is unknown – had a wall that was reinforced with towers and in many ways bore similarities to an ancient city laid out according to a plan, although the walls of the houses were still daubed with clay. The hill high above the city was once home to the Saluvii, an extremely warlike people whose repeated raids for booty drove the Greek colonists on the coast to desperation. Finally the point was reached when the merchants of Marseille had had as much as they could take and called on the Romans to help, as they themselves had little experience with conducting open warfare on land.

The Romans did not hesitate, and soon assembled an army: under the leadership of Consul Caius Sextinus Calvinus a crushing defeat was inflicted on the Saluvii in the year 123 BC, and Entremont was destroyed. Part of the population, including King Teutomalius, was able to flee in time; the rest of the Saluvii were enslaved. Contrary to the probable expectations of the Greeks, the victorious Romans resolved to found the first Roman town in Gaul at the foot of the Oppidum: "Aquae Sextiae Saluviorum," which is called Aix-en-Provence today.

Only two years later much of the south of France was declared a Roman province – hence the name Provence – and rapidly Romanised, although Greek influence remained noticeable for a long time.

Address 13100 Aix-en-Provence | Directions Aix-en-Provence is at the intersection of the A8 and A51. The Oppidum d'Entremont is three kilometres north of Aix on the D14. | Opening times Wed–Mon 9am–noon and 2–6pm, in winter until 5pm | Tip In the Musée Granet in Aix on Place Saint-Jean-de-Malte many finds (statues of warriors, skull trophies etc.) that were excavated in Entremont are on display. www.museegranet-aixenprovence.fr.

4__The Alyscamps
The world's most refined burial place

The Roman custom of burying the dead on the roads leading out of towns was not only practised in Italy – the Alyscamps in Arles also derives from this tradition.

Yet it was not until the first bishops of Arles, who laid down their lives for their faith, were interred along the Via Aurelia, that the Alyscamps (the name derives from the Elysian Fields [Allisii Camps] into which, according to ancient mythology, the souls of the blessed entered) gained in popularity in late antiquity.

The largest graveyard in Gaul, the Alyscamps was known all over Europe. Bereaved heirs sent the bodies of deceased relatives floating down the river Rhône in barrels and coffins so that they could find a final resting place in Arles. A gold coin placed between the teeth of the dead person served as a reward for those who salvaged the barrel and carried out the burial.

Those who could afford it had their mortal remains (or those of their family members) sent to Arles overland and buried in a stone sarcophagus.

Today the Alyscamps only covers a small part of its former extent. On either side of an avenue shaded by poplar and cypress trees, sarcophaguses dating from various periods are lined up one alongside the other. Originally grave lay next to grave over an area one and a half kilometres long, and in places the sarcophaguses were piled up one on top of another.

Nevertheless, the Alyscamps is still an enchanted place that has attracted many poets and artists such as Vincent van Gogh, who immortalised the avenue of tombs in four paintings. Hugo von Hofmannsthal called it "the most refined burial place in the world," and Rainer Maria Rilke was moved by the "soul-inhabited shade of the Alyscamps" with "graves that are open as if they were the graves of the resurrected."

Address Avenue des Alyscamps, 13200 Arles | **Directions** A 54, exit Arles. The Avenue des Alyscamps lies 500 metres southeast of the old quarter of town. | **Opening times** May–Sept daily 9am–7pm, Oct, March, April daily 9am–noon and 2–6pm, Nov–Feb 10am–noon and 2–5pm | **Tip** The most valuable sarcophaguses from the Alyscamps are on display in the Musée départemental Arles antique, Presqu'Île du Cirque Romain. Some of them had previously been put to other uses, as an altar or drinking trough.

5__Le Café la Nuit
A café like an oil painting

When the names van Gogh and Arles are mentioned in one breath, a whole panorama of pictures passes in front of the mind's eye. Like Monet and Giverny, van Gogh and Arles stand for a decisive moment in the history of modern art. When Vincent van Gogh got out of the train in Arles on 20 February 1888, he was immediately fascinated by the strong colours and light of the south. It was not long before the sun of Arles, as the art historian René Huyghe wrote, "had stung his brain, and he never again recovered." In the precisely 444 days that van Gogh spent in the city, he developed a new style that is generally regarded as typical of his work. The art world owes to his sojourn in Arles not only his countless depictions of sunflowers and the self-portrait with a bandaged ear and pipe, but also the painting "Terrasse du café le soir."

This picture of a café terrace in the evening, painted in September 1888, impresses the viewer with its intense colours, unusual perspectives and the motif of a starry sky. He painted it at the Place du Forum, where the Café la Nuit is still immediately recognisable today. However, it is not the original, but a reconstruction dating from the early 1990s, corresponding exactly to van Gogh's picture. The surroundings may have style and atmosphere, but unfortunately the café is nothing more today than a tourist trap serving mediocre food. In other words: don't drink more than a cup of coffee here in memory of van Gogh.

Not a popular man during his own lifetime, today van Gogh is one of the best-known representatives of the city. It is therefore hardly surprising that the practice of faking did not stop at the Café la Nuit: The drawbridge of Langlois (Pont de Langlois), which the artist painted, may have been preserved, but as a result of urgently needed construction work, it was moved by almost one kilometre.

Address 11, Place du Forum, 13200 Arles, tel. 0033/0490498330 | Directions A 54, exit to Arles. The Café la Nuit lies in the middle of the old quarter. | Tip A much better place to eat than the Café la Nuit is the restaurant Chez Caro, a down-to-earth bistro with scrubbed wooden tables on the opposite side of the square. Closed Tue and Wed; www.chezcaro.fr.

6__ The Cryptoporticus
An enigmatic underworld

Arles possesses many relics that testify to its Roman past. From the amphitheatre to the baths, these monuments are scattered all over the city. The most mysterious legacy of that era, however, lies hidden below the town hall: a cryptoporticus dating from the period around 40 BC, the purpose of which was a puzzle for a long time.

Its gloomy atmosphere is reminiscent of the catacombs in Rome. To be precise, the cryptoporticus of Arles is a subterranean, horse-shoe-shaped pillared structure of impressive dimensions: it consists of two double galleries almost 86 metres long, placed parallel to each other and connected by another gallery that is 59 metres long. The vaulted passageways, whose walls were covered with a thick layer of plaster impermeable to water, are eight and a half metres wide and almost four metres in height.

It was originally thought that this building was used as a storehouse or granary, but due to the narrowness of the entrances it is now believed that the structure was needed to even out differences in the ground level and thus to provide a solid foundation for the forum above.

As in other Roman cities, in Arles the forum was the centre of political, economic, cultural and religious life, and was constructed at the intersection of the two main streets. Today, apart from the cryptoporticus, only the remains of a temple built into the façade of the Hôtel Nord Pinus serve as reminders of the forum that once existed here.

A visit to this underworld is an opportunity to admire the capitals of a few columns in the dim light. More valuable finds such as a bearded head of Octavian and a votive shield are exhibited in the Musée de l'Arles Antique. The inscription on the votive shield has aroused speculation about whether a sanctuary in honour of Augustus may have stood on the forum.

Address Place de la République, 13200 Arles, access via the town hall | **Directions** A 54, exit to Arles. The town hall is in the middle of the old quarter. | **Opening times** May–Sept daily 9am–noon and 2–7pm, Oct, March, April daily 9am–noon and 2–6pm, Nov–Feb 10am–noon and 2–5pm | **Tip** It is worth buying a combined ticket (Pass Monuments), giving admission to all the sights.

7_ The Grand Hôtel Nord Pinus

Naked flesh and strong desires

The Grand Hôtel Nord Pinus still has an aura of something special. Since 1865 it has been the leading hotel in Arles, a place to stay that is truly redolent with history. Two Corinthian columns, which probably came from the portico of a temple, are integrated into the façade; while inside, heavy furnishings, mirrors adorned with gilding and other touches of pomp quickly convey a sense of its importance. The hotel lounge basks in the Art Deco charm of bygone days, a curving staircase with a wrought-iron balustrade leads up to the rooms, and the walls are decorated with old bull-fighting posters.

The illustrious list of former hotel guests includes Ernest Hemingway, Maria Callas, Curd Jürgens, Picasso, Jean Cocteau and Jean-Paul Sartre. To this can be added countless Spanish VIPs that are known only to insiders: during the "féria," the festival for tens of thousands of bull-fighting fans in April and September, room number 10, directly above the entrance, is traditionally reserved for the most famous torero, who, in the evening after the contest, acknowledges the ovations of spectators standing on the Place du Forum from the broad balcony, as Luis Miguel Dominguín once did. Dominguín was the uncrowned king of toreros in the 1940s and 1950s. Jean Cocteau spent sleepless nights longing for his dark eyes, and a picture on the wall of the room shows Cocteau in the company of the torero, sitting on the bed. But Dominguín preferred to spend his nights with the Hollywood actress Ava Gardner. In 1973 the celebrity photographer Helmut Newton chose this room to place Charlotte Rampling in front of a mirror with an elaborate golden frame on a dark wooden table. In the photograph the actress is completely naked, holding a glass of wine in her hand with her feet resting on an armchair. Her cool gaze over her shoulder seems to be directed at eternity.

Address 14, Place du Forum, 13200 Arles, tel. 0033/0490934444, www.nord-pinus.com |
Directions A 54, exit for Arles. The hotel is in the middle of the old quarter. | Tip It is
worth visiting the atmospheric hotel bar and restaurant, where many historic photos hang
from the walls. Closed Sunday and Monday.

8 — The Mistral Monument

A forgotten holder of the Nobel Prize for Literature

When they hear the word "mistral" in Provence, most travellers think of the famous downslope wind that blows through the Rhône valley, causing the temperature to plummet noticeably and bringing a radiant blue sky. The city fathers of Arles did not erect a monument to this infamous wind but to the poet Frédéric Mistral (1830–1914), who poses proudly on a plinth wearing a frock coat of bygone days. Today he has been almost completely forgotten beyond the borders of Provence, although he was by no means a provincial writer. In 1904 he was awarded the Nobel Prize for Literature (jointly with the Spanish dramatist J. Echegaray y Eizaguirre) for his epic of rural life, Mirèio (Mireille).

In Provence the memory of the poet is honoured to this day, as throughout his life he sought to preserve the Provençal language, which was dying out, by publishing not only magazines and almanacs but also a monumental dictionary. Instead of, "Quel est votre nom?" (What are you called?), in Provençal the phrase is, "Coume vous dison?" Or if you are as hungry as a wolf, you don't say: "J'ai une faim de loup," but "Ai lou ruscle."

Thanks to Mistral, Provençal long ago became an optional subject in schools again, and every sign at the entrance to a town or village shows the name in Provençal beneath the French place name.

Mistral used the money awarded with his Nobel Prize for the benefit of all: he spent it on enlarging and building an extension to the Museon Arlaten, of which he was a co-founder. This museum, housed in a venerable mansion in Arles, is filled to overflowing with a collection devoted to the everyday culture of Provence and its folk art, including all kinds of devotional items, costumes, paintings and products of the local craft tradition. For this achievement alone Frédéric Mistral deserved a monument.

Address Place du Forum, 13200 Arles | Directions A54, exit to Arles. The monument is in the middle of the historic quarter. | Opening times Museon Arlaten Tue–Sun 9.30am–12.30pm and 2–6pm, www.museonarlaten.fr | Tip In Maillanne, about 24 kilometres from Arles in the direction of Avignon, Frédéric Mistral's house is open to visitors.

9__ The Obelisk
Chariot races and sundials

Every day thousands of people walk across Place de la République in Arles without giving so much as a glance to a fountain adorned by an obelisk. Neither an inscription nor a plaque explains what this 15-metre-high pinnacle might be.

Arles, one of the most important Roman cities in ancient times, was called "Gaul's little Rome" (Gallula Roma). A population of more than 100,000 lived in Arles at the height of its prosperity. In accordance with an adage of those times, "bread and games," a circus for thrilling chariot races was of course part of the infrastructure of a big Roman city, as well as an amphitheatre. This "Cirque Romain" was situated in the southwest of Arles – close to today's Musée départemental Arles antique – and had imposing dimensions: with a length of approximately 450 metres and a width of 101 metres, the arena could accommodate more than 20,000 spectators.

Just as in the Circus Maximus in Rome, in Arles an obelisk stood at the centre of the spina and served as a stone marker at the turning point, forming a division between the two sides of the corso. It is not, by the way, an Egyptian obelisk; the red granite comes from the surroundings of Troy in Asia Minor. Some time after the 6th century, when the circus was no longer in use, the obelisk must have fallen over and broken into two pieces. Forgotten for centuries, it was re-erected in the centre of Arles in March 1676 and used as a sundial.

In honour of King Louis XIV a richly decorated sun globe was placed on the tip of the obelisk. The globe is now exhibited in the Musée Réattu.

The stone base on which the obelisk stands is adorned with bronze sculptures of lions; they are the work of Antoine Laurent Dantan, who created the elaborate fountain around the obelisk in the mid-19th century.

Address Place de la République, 13200 Arles | Directions A 54, exit to Arles. Place de la République is at the heart of the historic quarter. | Tip It is well worth visiting the Musée Réattu in Rue du Grand Prieuré, www.museereattu.arles.fr.

10__ The City Wall
39 towers and seven gates

There are not many cities in Europe whose historic centre is still surrounded by a city wall. Alongside York, Nuremberg and Lucca, Avignon is one of the few important medieval cities whose fortifications have survived almost completely. Its wall was broken open only in a few places in order to handle the increase in traffic. In the days when other cities, Vienna and Paris for example, tore down their defences and transformed the space this gained them into boulevards, Avignon had declined to the status of a provincial town, and there seemed to be no need to pull down its fortifications.

The ring of defensive walls was the outstanding characteristic of a late medieval town. It gave the inhabitants the highest possible degree of security. When the population increased, however, the walls had to be extended, as happened in Avignon for the last time between 1355 and 1370.

The orders to build this impressive monument were given by the popes, who wanted to protect their city from the grandes compagnies, roaming bands of mercenary soldiers several thousand strong. The course of the city wall was based on that of its Roman predecessor.

Only at its furthest north-western corner is the eight-metre-high fortification interrupted – by a rock, the Rocher des Doms, which serves as a natural wall. Everywhere else the wall was reinforced with 39 towers and also by a ditch, which has now been filled in; access to Avignon was controlled by seven city gates, which were once equipped with portcullises and drawbridges.

The best place from which to view the course of the city walls is the Rocher des Doms. In order to get an impression of the size and importance of medieval Avignon, take a walk around the town by following its ring of walls, which are almost four and a half kilometres long.

Address Place du Palais, 84000 Avignon | **Directions** A 7, exit to Avignon, parking spaces at the western edge of the city wall. | **Tip** Right in front of the city wall there is access to the Pont d'Avignon, famously celebrated in song.

11 Rue des Teinturiers
A cobble-stoned idyll

Avignon is a high-class, proud city: after all, popes once resided here with their complete entourages, from cardinals down to the usual hangers-on at court. It therefore comes as no surprise that the appearance of the city is characterised by countless churches and monasteries, as well as fine aristocratic mansions. Nevertheless, then as now there were also the common people, from the baker to the cobbler, who keep a city like Avignon alive and lend colour to it.

In many places, traces of the pre-industrial world have disappeared, but not in Rue des Teinturiers. The "street of the dyers," probably the loveliest lane in Avignon, runs directly alongside the channelled riverbed of the Sorgue, which is only two metres wide here and flows above ground. Old paddle wheels stand at the edge of the street as a reminder of the dyers' workshops that once existed here.

Today second-hand bookshops, a baker, several restaurants and cafés, as well as shops selling fabrics and antiques, have moved into the old workers' houses. Especially in the summer months, this alley, shaded by huge plane trees, is buzzing with life. Many students and occasionally a few tourists stroll along Rue des Teinturiers, sit on the low wall next to the river, and have a chat. The famous insect researcher Jean-Henri Fabre lived for a total of 16 years from 1855 in the little house at number 14, and received a visit from the philosopher John Stuart Mill. A solitary bell tower marks the site of a demolished Franciscan monastery, in which Laura, who was adored by the poet Petrarch, is said to have been buried.

This little street with its uneven cobblestones, which is free from motorised traffic, is at its most attractive in July during the renowned annual theatre festival, when it is the scene of lively activity until the early hours of the morning.

Address Rue des Teinturiers, 84000 Avignon | Directions A 7, exit to Avignon, parking spaces at the western edge of the city wall. Rue des Teinturiers is in the south-eastern part of the old quarter. | Tip On Rue des Teinturiers the chapel of the Grey Penitents is open to visitors all day.

12___ The TGV Station

Rushing southwards

TGV – this has been the magic word on French railways for more than 30 years. In 1981 the first "train à grande vitesse" went into service between Paris and Lyon. Since then the network has been continually extended. The connection to Marseille, which started operating in June 2001, is regarded as a milestone. On this classic route from Paris to the Mediterranean there were two famous long-distance trains, "Le Train Bleu" with its blue-and-gold painted luxury sleeping cars and the TEE Mistral, but not until the high-speed TGV service started up could the French railways offer a connection that was able to compete with air travel.

The TGV rushes through the Midi at racing speed, covering the 750 kilometres between the Gare de Lyon in Paris and Marseille in the amazing time of three hours and 20 minutes. To Avignon it takes only two hours and 37 minutes, reaching a top speed of 270 kilometres per hour along the way. Not even flying can beat that!

In order to avoid significant delays, the TGV station at Avignon, like the one for Aix-en-Provence, was not only planned as a through-station without connections to the rest of the rail network, but also constructed outside the city centre in both cases so that the trains would not need to slow down while passing through the city.

The architecture of the modern TGV stations is also appealing. The one in Avignon delights travellers with its spectacular 340-metre-long glass roof, slightly curved in a shape inspired by the up-turned hull of a ship.

Avignon and Aix-en-Provence are easily reached from London, too, with a trip through the Channel Tunnel on the Eurostar trains, which are based on the French TGV, taking less than three hours, followed by a short trek across Paris from the Gare du Nord to the Gare de Lyon – the total journey lasting between six and seven hours.

Address Chemin du Confluent, La Courtine, 84008 Avignon, www.gares-en-mouvement.com |
Directions The TGV station is three kilometres southwest of the city centre, well signposted. |
Tip From the TGV station, shuttle buses go to the centre of Avignon every 15 minutes.

13__ The Toilets at the Papal Palace

Nostalgia gives way to hygiene

"The French have almost always chosen the right place for their pissoirs. I remember one in Avignon next to the palace of the popes. Only a stone's throw from the charming square that seems to have been strewn with velvet and lace, masks and confetti on a spring night." In these words, Henry Miller, clearly delighted, recalled his stay in Avignon in the 1930s. The past master of erotic literature was even able to discover the poetic side of such banal matters as going to a public toilet.

The old, half-open "pissotières" with their metal-clad wooden channels, about which Miller enthused, vanished a long time ago and are no longer part of everyday life in France. Anyone who feels an all-too-human need in Avignon today, has a much harder time of it. Relieving themselves in the open air with a view of the Papal Palace is something that modern men should definitely avoid, despite the sublime view, or they will be a public nuisance. There are still some mouldy corners with a biting stink of urine, but it is advisable to look out for an up-to-date alternative that is also suitable for women: "sanisettes" is the French name for the public conveniences that have been appearing in cities for the last three decades. Although these toilet cubicles look as unwelcoming from outside as the walls of the Papal Palace and have no ambience at all, they are at least self-cleaning and can be locked from the inside.

The only alternative to the "sanisettes" is to go to one of the neighbouring cafés or the WCs in the palace itself, but these are only accessible to those who pay a steep admission price. Those in the know recommend the toilet at the Musée Réquien d'Histoire Naturelle: here admission is free, and you can learn about the flora and fauna of Provence at the same time.

Address Place du Palais, 84000 Avignon | **Directions** A 7, exit Avignon, parking spaces at the western edge of the city wall. | **Opening times** Musée Réquien June–Sept Wed–Mon 10am–6pm, Oct–May Tue–Sat 9am–noon and 2–6pm | **Tip** Le Grand Café is a cool café-restaurant, a little bit hidden away behind the Papal Palace at 4, Rue Sainte Anne. And it has toilets.

14 Brindille Melchio
Metre-long sausages

La Brindille Melchio is a small, inconspicuous sausage shop and delicatessen on the main square of Banon. Those who enter for the first time blink in astonishment: above the refrigerated counter hangs a veritable curtain of sausages that spans the whole width of the shop and emanates a truly seductive aroma.

These salami-like sausages, which are almost a metre long and no thicker than a finger, are the house speciality, known as brindilles, which means "straw" or "stalk." Brindilles are sold whole. They are available in several different flavours, some in shimmering pink, others covered in white flour. They are seasoned with either walnuts, pine nuts, spicy paprika, savory, juniper berries, cheese or even pastis. What a treat for the eye and the palate! As the sausages are perfectly hung and can be kept for several weeks, visitors can easily take them home at the end of a holiday.

In addition to his brindilles, Monsieur Melchio also sells delicious pasties, air-dried ham and home-made chestnut cream, as well as cheese, jam and lavender honey from Haute-Provence.

Don't fail to sample the Banon de Banon. This goat's cheese, known beyond the local area, is wrapped in chestnut leaves, tied up with bast fibre, and left to mature. Depending on its state of ripeness, it tastes mild and creamy, spicy or slightly acidic and is the size of a small plate. In 2003 Banon de Banon was awarded the honour of an "Appellation d'Origine Contrôlée" (AOC), a distinction that is restricted to just a few select types of cheese in France. The conditions of production are very strict: the milk has to come from free-grazing goats.

There is no better address in Haute-Provence for buying the ingredients for a picnic than La Brindille Melchio! And it doesn't take long to find an ideal spot to enjoy the picnic among the fields of lavender.

Address Place de la République, 04150 Banon, tel. 0033/0492732305 | Directions D950 between Sault and Forcalquier, in the middle of the town. | Opening times Daily 7.30am–12.30pm and 2.30–7pm, in July and August no lunch break. | Tip You can also order the sausages online. The postage costs for 10 brindilles are 46 euros; www.charcuterie-melchio.fr.

15__Librairie Le Bleuet
A true temple of books

The French bookshop trade is not in a good state of health. Online retailers and big chains such as Fnac have come to dominate the market. Owner-run bookshops can only be found in large towns and cities. In rural areas and in most small towns Maisons de la Presse, retail outlets that specialise in selling newspapers and magazines, also have the function of bookshops. Sometimes they are well stocked, and sometimes not.

In view of this it seems almost a miracle that the village of Banon, with a population of 1000, should have a bookshop at all. And Le Bleuet is not merely just another bookshop, but probably the most attractive in all Provence if not in the whole south of France. Local residents shook their heads in 1990 when Joël Gattefossé bought a papeterie and planned to convert and extend it to serve as a bookshop.

But the book enthusiast Gattefossé was not to be swayed from his course, and established what is a veritable shrine to books. An appealing wooden book tower next to the entrance invites passersby to come inside, where it is difficult to take everything in: the shelves are filled with almost 200,000 books, including more than 110,000 separate titles!

For a long time now Le Bleuet has drawn customers from far and wide – even from Aix-en-Provence and Nice. On average over 500 books a day are sold, as the wares range from cookbooks to ambitious literature.

As well as classics and modern literature, Provençal authors such as Jean Giono and Pierre Magnan are in great demand, and there is even a good selection of books in English. Joël Gattefossé was a good friend of Pierre Magnan; he often invited the author, who lived nearby in Forcalquier, to give readings in the shop, and all of Magnan's books are kept in stock.

Address Place Saint-Just, 04150 Banon | **Directions** D950 between Sault and Forcalquier, in the village centre. | **Opening times** Daily 9.15am–8pm | **Tip** Pierre Magnan's Death in the Truffle Wood (published by Vintage, 2006) is an exciting crime novel that is set in the woods around Banon.

16_ The Dragon
A monster in human form

If the legends are to be believed, Beaucaire suffered for centuries from the visitations of a man-eating monster, the drac, which claimed both maidens and knights as its victims. The dragon, which hid in the depths of the river Rhône, was invisible, but it could also take on human form.

One day it captured a washerwoman and forced her to raise its son. The woman is said to have been in its service for seven years, and then, to general astonishment, the dragon freed her. When the washerwoman some time later recognised the dragon in human form in the marketplace, it was reportedly seized with anger at being revealed and scratched out her eyes with its claws.

Beaucaire is a trading town with a long tradition on the right bank of the Rhône. The town was known all over Europe for its trade fair, beginning on 21 July each year, to which more than 100,000 visitors flocked in medieval times: the fair was free of taxes and duties, which made it a paradise for merchants and their customers. During this period many accidents occurred to shippers on the Rhône, which was the origin of the tale about the drac.

Beaucaire possesses buildings of great age, including fine burghers' houses – testimony to its wealth in days gone by. It is also worth visiting the Baroque church of Notre-Dame-des-Pommiers with a convex curve in its façade and the imposing town hall, which was constructed in classical style with three wings. A particularly attractive place to explore is the sleepy-looking district around Rue de la République and Place de la République, the town's most beautiful square where arcades and plane trees provide shade. It was once called Place Vieille.

Since 1988 the square has been the site of an outsized green sculpture of a dragon, a reminder of the legend of the creature that dwelled in the Rhône.

Address Place de la République, 30300 Beaucaire | Directions Beaucaire lies between Avignon and Arles on the right bank of the Rhône. Place de la République is in the middle of the old quarter. | Tip In memory of the monster, a dragon procession passes through the whole town for two days on the third weekend of June – a colourful spectacle, accompanied by crowds of children with lanterns.

17_L'Enclos des Bories
Shepherds' stone huts

Exploring the northern foothills of the Luberon, whether walking, cycling or driving, you cannot fail to come across semi-dilapidated stone huts, known as "bories." These circular structures, consisting of dry stone walls, look like an igloo or a bee-hive hut and are typical for the region.

Huts like this were built for thousands of years throughout the whole Mediterranean area. In Sardinia and Apulia they are known under the name "trulli," in Spain as "cabaños." The bories of Provence are more recent. The construction of this type of shelter probably did not begin here until the 17th century, even though the method of building is simple and gives the impression that the work dates from the Stone Age: without windows or the use of mortar, stones were piled up so that they supported each other and formed a vault-like roof. Access to the interior is given by an inconspicuous curved entrance. Very rarely was space made for a window-like opening.

Near to Bonnieux and Gordes there are larger groups of bories within a small area, which can be visited. While the "Village des Bories" near Gordes has been excessively smartened up to make it into a tourist attraction, the less visited "Enclos des Bories" close to Bonnieux has an appealingly original-looking character. Scattered across a lightly wooded terrain of cork oaks and olive trees, several dozen bories can be seen. They were once used as stalls for animals or as store chambers, but some of them were occupied by shepherds on a seasonal basis. Equipped with a simple plan of the site, which can be obtained at the entrance, you can explore them on your own.

At the far end of the Enclos des Bories you reach a kind of escarpment, from where there is a wonderful panoramic view of the surrounding villages and across the countryside as far as Mont Ventoux.

Address Quartier Le Rinardas, 84480 Bonnieux, www.enclos-des-bories.fr | **Directions** From Bonnieux two kilometres on the D 36 towards Lourmarin, then follow a woodland track on the right signed "Enclos des Bories." The area with the bories is situated beyond the campsite and can be reached on foot from there. | **Opening times** April–Oct daily 10am–7pm | **Tip** In Bonnieux there is a small and interesting bakery museum, the Musée de la Boulangerie, on Place de la République.

18 Historic Advertising

In search of lost brands

As far as consumption and advertising are concerned, France took its cue from America long ago. Huge supermarkets have sprung up at the edge of every little town, and tills with bar-code scanners have been standard for two decades even in the remotest mountain villages. Everything that is to be sold also has to be advertised: annoyingly and aggressively on the radio, loudly and colourfully on billboards.

It is a pleasant contrast to see the historic façade advertising that catches the eye from time to time on the walls of Provençal buildings – faded, nostalgia-inducing testimony to days when the world of products was simpler. It was not every week that a new motif was painted on a wall. If you walk through the streets with your eyes peeled, you will discover these "murs réclames" again and again. Some façades were painted over several times. Here and there the plaster is crumbling, and on some buildings windows were even cut out of the advertising space.

"Murs réclames" are an open-air museum of vanished brands and products. Who today has heard of a paint manufacturer called Ripolin or a detergent called Crème Éclipse? Colourful advertisements first shone out from walls in the late 19th century. This form of advertising had its heyday in the 1930s and 1950s. Along with banks like Crédit Lyonnais and newspapers like Le Petit Marseillais, it was, above all, the makers of alcoholic drinks such as Ricard and Suze who spread their message on the sides of buildings. Campaigns for aperitifs like Cinzano and Byrrh were especially common. The uncrowned king of the "murs réclames" was Dubonnet, a company that always used the slogan, "Du bo, du bon, dubonnet," and a conspicuous shade of blue for its "vin tonique." The arrival of modern mass media brought new forms of advertising, and the colourful old façades are now decaying.

Address Rue République, 83170 Brignoles | Directions Brignoles lies on the A 8 between Aix-en-Provence and Fréjus. Rue République is to the west of the old quarter. | Tip Stéphane Mallet has written a book about Provençal "murs réclames" illustrated with many photos; www.mallet.fr.

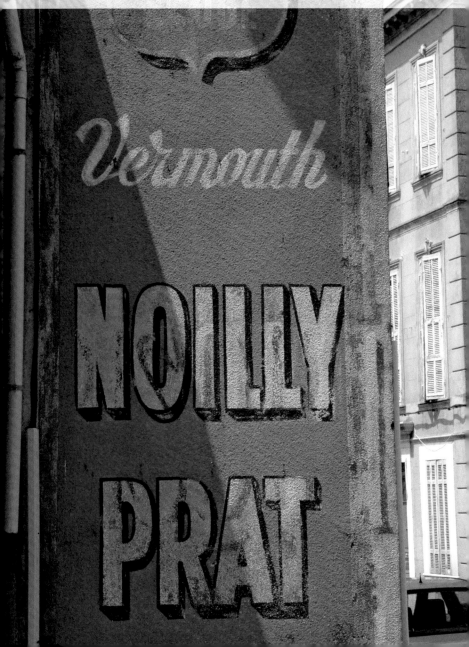

19 ___ The Flood Wall
Worse than Hannibal

Many cities in Provence, for example Avignon, Aix-en-Provence and Arles, are or were protected by a strong wall. Caderousse on the left bank of the Rhône has a uniquely robust, almost circular wall that completely surrounds the little town and is interrupted in only two places to provide access.

Caderousse is a historic place, as well. Hannibal is said to have crossed the Rhône here in 218 BC with an army of 50,000 warriors, 10,000 horses and 37 elephants under his command. However, the city wall was not built to keep out hordes of enemies. The attacks that afflicted Caderousse were the recurring floods of the largest river in France, the Rhône. Every few years it overflowed its banks and not only inundated the pastures and meadows of local farmers but also damaged the houses of the town.

In November 1840 more than 80 buildings were almost destroyed, and the flooding was especially bad on 31 May 1856, when all the houses in the town were under water as high as the second floor. The flood left behind a field of rubble and devastation. Most dwellings were uninhabitable for months. To get a sense of just how high the water rose on that occasion, take a look at the classical-style town hall, on which the various water levels have been marked – an impressive sight.

After this catastrophe, on the initiative of two agricultural engineers, work was undertaken to construct a flood wall, in order to give Caderousse and its 3,100 inhabitants permanent protection against further damage.

Within the space of three years a wall was built around the town – more than 1700 metres long and nine metres high. The two openings in the wall that provide access to the town can be blocked up quickly in case of emergency. Should such a thing occur, Caderousse would lie amidst the floodwaters of the Rhône like an island.

Address 84860 caderousse | Directions caderousse lies on the d 17, about eight kilometres southwest of orange. | Tip you can take a walk on the flood defences of caderousse and easily stroll around the town in less than half an hour.

20 The Friday Market

A veritable feast for the senses

One of the most impressive experiences on a journey to Provence is to spend some time at a market. The stalls are truly a feast for all the senses! Lettuce, fruit and vegetables are piled up artistically to form cascades. The aroma of ripe cheese made from unpasteurised milk and fresh bread makes your mouth water.

And one thing is for certain: even though a market is held in every town and every village in Provence, none of them can compete with the range of products and the atmosphere of the market at Carpentras. Each Friday morning the town seems to be bursting at the seams. The roads leading into Carpentras are congested and parking spaces hard to find. Beneath the plane trees in Avenue Victor Hugo and throughout the historic quarter of the town, one market stall is lined up next to another. More than 300 traders come here every week to offer their wares. They erect the stalls in the early hours of the morning and start to decorate them creatively with fresh produce.

It is like walking around a gigantic open-air supermarket: printed fabrics, household goods, soap, arts and crafts, fashion and second-hand clothes are all on offer.

However, the attention of visitors is mainly directed to edible treats: in addition to one stall after another selling fruit and vegetables, there are some that offer more than a dozen kinds of potatoes, goat's cheese from Banon, salami with a pepper crust, ham from Avignon, fresh seafood and snails.

It goes without saying that shoppers can sample all kinds of different honey and olive oil from a variety of regions, or taste wines. The cooked-food stalls send out seductive signals: the smells of grilled chicken drumsticks, paella from huge pans and freshly made pizza fill the air. No one should fail to visit the biggest market in Provence!

Address 84200 Carpentras (town centre) | Directions Carpentras lies to the east of Avignon and can be reached via the D 942 in half an hour. | Tip The market in Provence that gets the most visitors is the Foire de la Saint Siffrein. It is held on 27 November in and around the whole old quarter of Carpentras in conjunction with a big market for livestock.

21 Passage Boyer

Strolling through a job-creation programme

Writers such as Walter Benjamin and Louis Aragon sang the praises of the famous shopping arcades in Paris that were built in the mid-19th century to allow citizens to stroll around the city and do their shopping even in bad weather: "The arcades are a centre for trade in luxury goods. Their fittings place art in the service of commerce. The Parisians of the day do not tire of admiring them," wrote Benjamin.

The shopping arcades of the French capital may be famous, but it is not widely known that people in the provincial town of Carpentras also dreamed of having one. It seems probable that the eponymous Jean Boyer had this idea in his head when he came back from a visit to Paris and succeeded in convincing the town council to carry out his plan. After the revolution of 1848 a "street of glass" almost 100 metres long was erected close to the marketplace and the Rue des Halles, which is lined by medieval arcades. The iron-and-glass construction named Passage Boyer was built as part of a job-creation programme, as it was largely made by unemployed labourers in national workshops. The results were greeted with astonishment all over Provence: a high-class temple of shopping with two dozen stores, including boutiques, hat-makers, cafés and antiquarian books – not even Avignon had anything like that!

Unfortunately Passage Boyer now looks a little neglected. Some stores are in danger of remaining empty, as shoppers have stayed away in recent times and a thorough renovation has not been carried out. Instead of window-shopping in this charming glass-covered street, most of the inhabitants of Carpentras prefer to buy their shirts and trousers in the big shopping centres on the edge of town. These places may be ugly, but prices are low and parking spaces plentiful there. Carpentras lacks the well-to-do clientele that flocks to the high-class boutiques of Paris.

Address Passage Boyer, 84200 Carpentras | **Directions** Carpentras lies to the east of Avignon and can be reached via the D942 in half an hour. Passage Boyer is in the middle of the old part of town. | **Tip** In Carpentras there is a covered swimming pool dating from the 1930s: Piscine Couverte in Rue du Mont de Piété.

22 __ The Synagogue
Hidden behind an inconspicuous façade

A papal enclave, the Comtat Venaissin, existed for centuries in Provence. After the end of the Albigensian Wars, i.e. even before the popes went into exile in Avignon in 1309, the counts of Toulouse had donated lands to the papacy on the east bank of the Rhône. This territory, which roughly corresponds to the Département Vaucluse today, was administered from Carpentras from 1320 onwards. In contrast to the situation in neighbouring parts of France, no taxes had to be paid and no military service was required in the Comtat Venaissin, and furthermore Jews who were under the protection of the pope were permitted to settle in the county – a right of which they made good use in Cavaillon and L'Isle-sur-la-Sorgue, as well as in Carpentras.

The Jewish community in Carpentras is one of the oldest in France; in the late 14th century it already had about 2000 members – which meant that one in ten of the residents of the town were Jewish. The community lived crowded together in a ghetto that existed until the French Revolution.

The synagogue, which once lay in the middle of the densely built ghetto and today stands on the edge of the Place de l'Hôtel de Ville, is regarded as one of the finest in Provence.

Its relatively inconspicuous façade offers no clue to the fact that the first floor of the building holds a large, light-flooded place of worship with wonderful Rococo fittings, including a starry blue vault, wooden panelling and wrought-iron grilles. There is a tabernacle for the torah rolls and a throne of the prophet Elijah. Furthermore an assembly room, the entrance to the women's synagogue and a bakery for unleavened bread are grouped around a courtyard behind the building. In the basement there is also a Jewish ritual bath (mikvah), which is fed with spring water according to Hebrew rites.

Address Place de l'Hôtel de Ville, 84200 Carpentras | **Directions** Carpentras lies to the east of Avignon and can be reached via the D 942 in half an hour. The synagogue is in the town centre. | **Opening times** Tours Mon – Thu at 10, 10.30, 11, 11.30am, 3, 3.30, 4 and 4.30pm, Fri 10.30, 11, 11.30am, 3 and 3.30pm | **Tip** In Carpentras there is a 16th-century Jewish cemetery. It can be visited only by making application to the Office de Tourisme; www.carpentras-ventoux.com.

23__ The Calanque d'En-Vau

The emerald-green bay of your dreams

Fortunately the most beautiful bays on the French Mediterranean coast can only be accessed by walking or by taking a boat. One of them is the Calanque d'En-Vau, which, with its shimmering, emerald-coloured water has everything that it takes to be described as a dream bay. It can be reached comfortably in an hour or so from Cassis on a long-distance trail marked in white and red – though at the end a short but extremely steep descent has to be made. Sturdy shoes are therefore recommended.

Calanques, which are cut like fjords into the limestone rock, were once river valleys. The name comes from the Provençal word "calanco," which means something like "falling steeply." Climatic changes at the end of the Ice Age resulted in a rise in sea level; about 10,000 years ago the sea was therefore able to penetrate far into the river valleys. This was the origin of the calanques that are found between Cassis and Marseille.

In order to preserve the unique character of this coastal strip with its variety of rare plants and animals (for example Bonelle's eagle, the peregrine falcon and the emerald lizard), in 2012 it was designated the Parc National des Calanques.

Out of the half a dozen bays found in this region, the Calanque d'En-Vau with its wonderful pebble beach is the most spectacular. Do not fail to take your swimming gear with you, as the crystal-clear water is extremely tempting.

The rocks to left and right, eaten away by erosion, are popular with climbers. On slender pinnacles of rock like "God's finger" the freeclimbers seem to defy gravity effortlessly, and hang from the rock more than fifty metres above the sea. There is no place for refreshments, so visitors have to bring along their own food and drink for a beach picnic! And it goes without saying that litter has to be taken away afterwards.

Address 13260 Cassis | Directions A 50, exit to Cassis. Parking spaces are scarce in the town centre, so it is best to head for one of the car parks and pay the fee. The calanques lie to the west of the harbour. From Calanque de Port-Miou a long-distance path leads to Calanque d'En-Vau. | Tip Several times daily from 9am until 6pm, boats leave from the Quai Saint-Pierre in Cassis and head for the calanques; but they are not allowed to moor there.

24 __ The Corniche des Crêtes
Dizzying prospects

After only a few hundred metres the engine starts to complain loudly, as the 15-kilometre-long Corniche des Crêtes, which runs from Cassis to La Ciotat, begins with a 30 percent gradient so that drivers need to stay in first gear to handle the ascent and its hairpin bends. But it is worth making the effort, as the cliff coast between the two towns is renowned as one of the most beautiful in the Mediterranean region!

To the left and right of the Corniche des Crêtes, a barren rocky landscape rises to the cliffs. Along the road, which often runs right next to the edge, there are several places to park a car and stop at viewing points. An especially spectacular stop is at Cap Canaille, the highest cliff in France at 363 metres. Here the view across the sea and the bay of Cassis, extending as far as the Île de Riou, is breathtaking!

However, visitors should beware of sudden gusts of wind and the danger of crumbling rock, and shouldn't get too near to the edge of the cliffs. When the mistral is blowing, it can even take strength to get out of the car. On especially windy days, the road is closed to traffic on account of the danger of fire.

Apart from admiring the view over the sea, it is worth taking a look at the vegetation, even though this is mostly confined to shrubs, primarily rock roses and gorse. Here and there a few small fir trees grow.

To reach the highest elevation, the Grande Tête (394 metres), which lies a little back from the cliff edge, it is necessary to walk. A last stop leads to the 328-metre-high Sémaphore du Bec de l'Aigle, a signal station remaining from the time of Napoleon. Here a map board gives information about the range of mountains that runs between Marseille and Toulon. Beyond this point, the road descends again steeply to reach the port of La Ciotat.

Address Between 13260 Cassis and 13600 La Ciotat | Directions The Corniche des Crêtes is the D141 road. | Tip You can walk from Cassis to La Ciotat on a trail marked in yellow in about three and a half hours. A bus takes you back again.

25 Notre-Dame-du-Roc
The chapel on the sugarloaf

Whichever way you enter Castellane, you cannot miss the sight of the massive monolithic rock that rises directly behind the little town. Castellane with its Marcel-Sauvaire marketplace and lots of cafés undoubtedly has its charms, but sooner or later the urge comes to climb the mountain crowned by the Chapelle Notre-Dame-du-Roc.

Passing the remains of the late medieval city wall, a footpath called the Chemin de Croix leads up to the rock that towers above Castellane in a shape reminiscent of a sugarloaf. It takes about half an hour to do the ascent of almost 200 metres. The hotter the weather and the more plentiful the sweat on your forehead, the more often you wonder if you should reconsider the decision to go up, and which mad custom lies behind the idea that a chapel has to stand on top of every conspicuous mountain. Once you have reached the summit of the 903-metre rock, the reward is an overwhelming view across the mountain ranges of Haute-Provence and the roofs of Castellane.

The small pilgrims' chapel of Notre-Dame-du-Roc, decorated with a statue of the Virgin Mary, dates from the 18th century and was constructed on the foundations of a Romanesque predecessor. In the Middle Ages a settlement named Petra Castellana stood atop the rock. In 1703 it was destroyed, along with the castle and church, during the wars of religion.

The church interior is adorned with numerous votive gifts and plaques, including thanks given by a man rescued after shipwreck and a prisoner of war who was liberated. It is especially worth admiring a plaque dating from 1835 that depicts a procession of the "Pénitents blanc": More than 100 penitents clad in white habits are walking up to the chapel in a long, snaking line in order to pray for the deliverance of Castellane and its region from cholera.

Address 04120 Castellane | Directions Castellane is on the Route Napoléon (N 85) between Grasse and Digne-les-Bains. There are plenty of parking spaces in the town centre. | Tip From Castellane you can undertake rafting tours on the Verdon; www.rafting-castellane.com.

26 The Roman Garden

With a pool thrown in

As part of the Roman Empire, Provence was given a network of out-standing infrastructure, including roads, bridges and aqueducts. It also received Roman culture, with its amphitheatres, temples and baths. Opulent gardens with fountains were part of this new way of life.

It is not difficult to understand that the shelf life of a garden is shorter than that of a temple or a triumphal arch. Although, with the help of aerial photography, archaeologists have succeeded in recent years in locating the foundations of Roman villas in various places and partly excavating them; usually only large agricultural estates have been found in this way.

It had been known for a long time that a luxurious Roman villa from the reign of Emperor Augustus once stood above Caumont-sur-Durance, but it was not until 1998 that archaeologists succeeded in identifying the remains of an extensive garden that belonged to the villa in late antiquity – although no structures worth mentioning that testified to the villa itself have been preserved.

With great commitment and enthusiasm a Roman garden was laid out according to authentic examples and opened in 2006. On an area of 12,000 square metres the Jardin Romain provides insights into Roman horticulture and mythology.

The site is organised according to themes – individual sections are, for example, dedicated to the gods Jupiter and Apollo. A flower garden, a vegetable patch and a labyrinth were also created. In the middle of the garden is a pool, 65 metres long and more than three metres wide, serving as an eye-catcher at the centre of the site. It is the largest Roman pond in all of France, and great efforts were made in its design: the bottom was paved with 55,000 small bricks. The master of the house could walk into his pool down a monumental flight of steps.

Address 84510 Caumont-sur-Durance, www.jardin-romain.fr | **Directions** Caumont-sur-Durance is on the A7, three kilometres east of the exit to Avignon East. The garden lies above Caumont on Rue du Général de Gaulle and is well signposted. | **Opening times** June–Sept daily 10am–12.30pm and 3–7pm, April, May, Oct Wed–Mon 2–6pm, Feb, March, Nov daily except Wed–Mon 2–5pm | **Tip** Directly above the Jardin Romain stands the 12th-century Chapelle Saint-Symphorien.

27 __ The Wine Village
The papal vineyard

The name Châteauneuf-du-Pape alone has a mystic ring that makes the eyes of wine lovers shine, as it is regarded as the king of wines from southeast France. Although cultivating vines was one of the outstanding cultural achievements of the ancient Greeks and Romans, alongside building amphitheatres and temples, in the end it was the popes in Avignon who made the reputation of

Châteauneuf-du-Pape. Clement V and John XXII especially promoted the cultivation of grapes on the hills below their summer residence.

Châteauneuf-du-Pape owes its exceptional quality to, among other things, the dry gravelly soil on which its grapes grow. The stones, which were once washed here by the Rhône, store the sun's warmth during the day and pass it on to the vines at night. This gives the grapes a particularly high degree of ripeness. The alcohol content is at least 12.5 percent, in good vintages sometimes as high as 15.5 percent. A further guarantee of the quality of Châteauneuf-du-Pape is that wine farmers are restricted to a maximum yield of 35 hectolitres per hectare of vineyard, which necessarily leads to the rejection of grapes of poor quality. A characteristic unique in all France is that a total of 13 different varieties of grape are permitted, although it is principally Grenache, Mourvèdre and Syrah that are cultivated. As almost 96 percent of the harvest is sold in the form of strong cuvée red wine, not many people know that good, long-lasting white wines are also made in Châteauneuf-du-Pape.

Full-bodied and fruity thanks to the Grenache grape, the wines have a low tannin content, which means that they can be drunk relatively quickly. On the other hand, even the lowest-priced Châteauneuf-du-Pape wines can easily be stored for ten years. The very best can lie in the cellar twice as long and are sold for three-figure sums.

Address 84230 Châteauneuf-du-Pape | Directions Châteauneuf-du-Pape is 15 kilometres north of Avignon on the D 17. | Tip Try the wines from 1990, 1995, 1998, 1999, 2001 and 2007: they are regarded as great vintages.

28__ The Village Pond

Shaded by plane trees

Cucuron, on the south slopes of the Luberon, is one of those Provençal picture-postcard villages that immediately melts the heart of every single visitor. The houses with their landscape of jumbled roofs nestle around a massive church like a flock huddling around the shepherd. There are still castle walls with a ruined keep and the remains of a town wall with its gateways. This is a village with a patina.

No wonder the location scouts of the film industry long ago discovered that Cucuron makes an authentic backdrop. It started in 1986 with "Jean Florette," a film based on a novel by Marcel Pagnol starring Gérard Depardieu and Yves Montand in the leading roles. Scenes from the film version of Jean Giono's "The Hussar on the Roof" with Juliette Binoche were also shot in Cucuron, and more recently it was the setting for a scene of the movie "A Good Year" based on a book by Peter Mayle, in which Russell Crowe tries his luck as a wine grower in Provence.

Cucuron has many picturesque corners, but the nicest spot is a man-made pond bordered by stone walls. Surrounded by ancient, knotty plane trees whose smooth grey-green bark has split open in places, it lies on the north edge of the village. Like outsized candelabras with many arms, the crowns of the trees rise to the sky and are reflected in the dull shine of the standing water. The dense foliage dims the power of the sun and bathes the scene in a soft, almost milky light.

The long pond is in fact an early industrial monument, as it was built in the 16th century to power a watermill by means of an underground channel. If you would like to enjoy the peaceful atmosphere here, the best place to sit is in one of the two restaurants with a view of the pond – or the window of a room in the neighbouring hotel.

Address Place de l'Étang, 84160 Cucuron | **Directions** North of Aix-en-Provence via the D62 and D56. Place de l'Étang borders the north part of the old quarter. | **Tip** La Petite Maison de Cucuron is by far the best restaurant in Cucuron; www.lapetitemaisondecucuron.fr.

29___ The Lace Peaks
A walk across striking mountains

Among the many mountain ranges that cross Provence from east to west, the Dentelles de Montmirail stand out thanks to their conspicuous shape. Directly adjacent to Mont Ventoux, between Gigondas and Malaucène, rises a massif that is visible from far away. The name "Dentelles" is a reference to its unusual form, which is reminiscent of lace. The pointed peaks of this limestone range, prettily shaped by erosion, are, however, much less high than the summit: at 730 metres, Mont Saint Armand is the highest point in this mountain range. It can quickly be reached from the little village of Suzette.

The Dentelles range, a little over ten kilometres in length, is regarded as an ideal region for walkers. The steep rock walls form an attractive contrast to the Mediterranean vegetation, which is interspersed with extensive vineyards and fruit orchards. On pinnacles such as the Dentelles Sarrasines, freeclimbers test their skills in conquering the naked rock.

Visitors who are interested in culture take the walk from Lafare via a little road to the Romanesque church of Saint-Christophe. Yet another Romanesque chapel can be discovered on the southern foothills of the Notre-Dame-d'Aubusson. This small church was built about 1000 years ago, but so badly damaged during the wars of religion that it later served as a stable for horses. Under the circumstances, it is fortunate that the folk-art-style mural paintings inside the chapel have survived the centuries.

On the west side of the Dentelles de Montmirail, where the massif falls away towards the river Rhône, lie some of the very best sites in all of Provence for cultivating vines. The resonant names of Gigondas, Beaumes-de-Venise, Séguret, Sablet, Rasteau and Vacqueyras stand for excellent red wines that are for the most part fruity and extremely full-bodied.

Address 84190 Dentelles de Montmirail | Directions North of Carpentras between the
D 8 and the D 938. | Tip A few minutes' walk north of Lafare you can refresh yourself in
the Cascade du Ravin, a small waterfall.

30__ The Gassendi Monument
A Provençal philosopher

Dressed in a flowing gown with his head slightly lowered, the most famous son of Digne-les-Bains stands on a stone plinth: the philosopher and natural scientist Pierre Gassendi. To be precise he was born in Champtercier, a small village a few kilometres west of Digne, the son of a farmer, on 22 January 1592. However, the capital of the Alpes-de-Haute-Provence department is so proud of Gassendi that it set up a monument to him here in Digne, and named the boulevard of the old quarter, laid out as a showcase street, in his honour in the 19th century.

"Who was Pierre Gassendi?" some will ask. As a child Pierre attracted attention with his quickness to grasp things and his linguistic skills; patrons supported him, and he became a teacher of rhetoric at the age of only 16. After studying theology and being consecrated as priest, in 1616 he was appointed professor of philosophy in Aix-en-Provence. However, he returned to Digne-les-Bains to be dean of the cathedral that rises behind his monument. Here he devoted himself to a variety of scientific studies. He was the first man to formulate a kind of law of thermodynamics.

Gassendi engaged in lively correspondence not only with Descartes and Thomas Hobbes, but also with many other scholars of his day. On the basis of these exchanges of letters he composed many biographies, for example of Tycho Brahe, Regiomontanus and Nicholas Copernicus.

As an astronomer, too, Gassendi did pioneering work. He spent many a night observing the heavens on the summit of Cousson, which is situated southwest of Digne-les-Bains. His observations of the planet Mercury proved Galileo's assertion that the sun stands at the centre of our planetary system.

Gassendi spent the last years of his life as professor at the Collège de France in Paris, where he died in 1655 after a long illness.

Address Place Général de Gaulle, 04000 Digne-les-Bains | Directions N85 between
Grasse and Sisteron. Boulevard Gassendi leads straight to Place Général de Gaulle, both in
the town centre. | Tip Musée Gassendi is an appealing museum of art and natural history
that also provides information about Gassendi's work; www.musee-gassendi.org.

31 Station Tcheka
Fill up on fashion

Paris is the city of fashion and haute couture – no question about that. Since the time of Coco Chanel, trend-setting designers have been worshipped like demi-gods in France, as the famous Parisian chic is more than just a symbol of elegance – it also stands for permissive freedom. Yet long ago, suitability for everyday wear took precedence over the wish for exclusivity. The latest trends in fashion are now primarily dictated by those who literally take them from the catwalk onto the street.

The fashion business and good taste are at home on the Seine; here the latest designs by Yves Saint-Laurent, Christian Lacroix, Jean-Paul Gaultier and Dior are celebrated at the annual fashion shows. In this respect, Provence is truly provincial. The region is more associated with yellow-and-blue tablecloths than with cool trends. Fortunately, however, there are a few exceptions. One glimmer of light is the Tcheka fashion label, founded in Marseille in 1998 by Nicolas Douyer.

Tcheka's stylish clothes are now sold in more than 200 boutiques around the world – as well as in a slightly strange location off the beaten track in the west of Marseille. Here, in the hinterland of the Côte Bleue, the label has opened an unusual concept store, called Station Tcheka.

The ambience alone, an abandoned petrol station dating from the 1970s, is fascinating. Between disused petrol pumps and tyre stands, casual dresses, blouses and shirts from the latest Tcheka collection and from other trendy designers are sold at comparatively reasonable prices.

The workshop atmosphere is authentic, and there is also a hairdressing salon and a little café to go with the clothing and accessories. No wonder Station Tcheka has become a rendezvous for the "jeunesse dorée."

Address 52, Route de Rove, 13820 Ensuès-la-Redonne, www.tcheka.fr | Directions Station Tcheka is on the eastern edge of Ensuès-la-Redonne on the D5, which leads to Marseille. | Opening times April–Sept Wed–Sun 10am–7pm and Mon, Tue noon–7pm, Oct–March Wed–Sat 10am–1pm and 4–7pm | Tip A side trip to the sea at La Redonne is a must.

32 — Chapelle Saint-Michel-de-Cousson

A Météora monastery in Provence

A few die-hard Bonapartists are still to be found in France. Some of them make a pilgrimage through Provence in the footsteps of the great Emperor Napoleon, and thus reach the end of the valley where the remote, 100-person hamlet of Entrages is situated. On his spectacular return from Elba to Paris, the self-proclaimed emperor of the French crossed the Col de Corobin and stopped in Entrages on 4 March 1815, before continuing his triumphant march via Digne-les-Bains and Grenoble.

All other visitors who find their way to Entrages have come to see the Chapelle Saint-Michel-de-Cousson. To view the solitary little chapel, you first have to make an arduous ascent of some 500 metres. The mountain named Cousson is part of the Trois-Évêchés massif, which rises a few kilometres south of Digne-les-Bains. A well-signposted trail marked in yellow and red leads to it – up to the Pas d'Entrages, then through mixed woodland to a forest house. From there you follow the yellow markings towards the summit of Cousson, the elevation on which the polymath scholar Pierre Gassendi made his astronomical observations. However, the route passes around Cousson on a rock edge that juts out of the woods like a cliff. Walking across a pasture, after almost two and a half hours you reach a mountain ridge on whose northern outcrop stands the Chapelle Saint-Michel.

The church here was built in the 11th century by monks from the Abbaye Saint-Victor in Marseille, and in its exposed position is a little bit reminiscent of the Metéora monasteries in Greece. Except on one single day of the year, Whit Monday, when a pilgrimage to the chapel takes place, this is a quiet and peaceful spot. The steps are a wonderful place to rest and enjoy the view of the mountain peaks of Haute-Provence.

Address 04000 Entrages | Directions Via the D 20 from Digne-les-Bains. The walk starts at the car park above the village. | Tip Between Entrages and Digne lie the springs of the thermal bath Les Eaux Chaudes, which is open from mid-February until early December; www.eurothermes.com.

33__ The Château Park
A horticultural jewel

The Haut-Var region is a thinly populated territory with sleepy little villages and natural beauty on all sides, which earns it the name "Provence Vert" (Green Provence). In the middle of the Haut-Var lies the hamlet of Entrecasteaux, consisting of just a few dozen houses that huddle at the foot of the castle hill. Since Entrecasteaux was founded, the village and castle have been one inseparable entity. Until the French Revolution the lord of the castle was also the patron of the village.

The present-day château of Entrecasteaux stands on the foundations of a medieval castle. When the Count of Grignan was appointed governor general of Provence in 1670, he built himself a fine summer residence in Entrecasteaux to replace the crumbling castle ruins.

Having admired the impressive gardens of the palaces at Vaux-le-Vicomte and Versailles during several visits to Paris, he gave a commission to the Sun King's gardener. And thus it came about that André le Nôtre (1613–1700) designed a garden "à la française" in Provence, even though it was a small one.

Geometrical lines of perspective, precisely clipped hedges and magnolia trees are an essential part of the garden, as are fountains with jets of water – after all, in the Baroque age, the purpose of a garden was to extend the living apartments of the noble classes out into nature.

During the turbulent era of the French Revolution, the château and gardens of Entrecasteaux became increasingly dilapidated, however. After falling into decay for many years, the château was purchased in 1974 by a Scottish eccentric named Ian McGarvie-Munn and restored, a task which took decades to complete. Since then, the gardens beneath the château, which are now freely accessible, have been returned to their old glory.

Address 83570 Entrecasteaux, www.chateau-entrecasteaux.com | **Directions** Entrecasteaux is eight kilometres south of Salernes on the D 31. The château is in the middle of the village. | **Opening times** Only as part of a guided tour: Sun–Fri 4pm, in August additionally Sun 11,30am | **Tip** Bistro Gourmande at the foot of the château is a pleasant place to dine. Closed Monday and Tuesday

34 The Étang de Berre
The largest salt lake in Provence

Large salt lakes, of which there are dozens, are a typical feature of the Rhône delta and the French Mediterranean coast of Languedoc. With a surface area of 15,500 hectares, the Étang de Berre is the largest of these lakes in the south of France. Nevertheless, few tourists find their way to the lake. Almost no one is to be found on the shore of the Étang de Berre, least of all bathers.

To be exact, it is a lake of brackish water that is only about ten metres deep, fed by several small watercourses and the sea. The only natural connection between the étang and the Mediterranean is the Canal de Caronte, which flows through Martigues and Port-de-Bouc, the "Venice of Provence".

Excavations and archaeological finds have shown that the shores of the Étang de Berre were settled as early as the Bronze Age. The first humans here were mainly engaged in fishing, and extracting salt in primitive salt works. The earliest towns were not founded until Greek and Roman times. Martigues, on the south bank of the lake, is one of the oldest towns in Provence.

Today the Étang de Berre is primarily associated with industrial plants built in the 20th century. Many companies and enormous re-fineries were established here, especially on the flat east bank, to take advantage of the proximity to Marseille. The Canal de Caronte was deepened to enable large tankers to sail through the lake. In 1922 Marseille airport was opened on the eastern shore. It is no wonder that the lake's fragile ecosystem lost its equilibrium. By the 1970s the Étang de Berre was as good as dead.

Measures to protect its ecosystem have improved the situation considerably since then. Water treatment plants were built and actions were taken to restore the lake to its natural condition. Fishing has now started again on the shores of the Étang de Berre, mainly for eels, but also for sea bream.

Address Étang de Berre | Directions Via the A 55 from Marseille. The motorway ends in Martigues, which lies on the lake. | Tip Near the little town of Saint-Mitre-les-Remparts there is a circular trail marked in yellow with information panels that explain the flora and fauna of the salt lake.

35__ The Source of the Sorgue
The world's deepest spring basin

The sources of rivers are almost always surrounded by a mystical aura. This applies especially to the source of the Sorgue, which flows out of the limestone mountains from beneath a massive rock wall, a few hundred metres from Fontaine-de-Vaucluse. Back in Roman times people made their way to the source and threw a few coins in, hoping that fate would smile on them. They probably puzzled over the depth of the spring even in those days.

The first known scientific dive was made in 1878, when a dock worker from Marseille, Nello Ottonelli, swam down 23 metres into the spring, which has a temperature of 12 degrees Celsius. The famous deep-sea explorer Jacques Cousteau made a number of dives, but failed each time to reach the bottom: in his first attempt in 1946 he descended to a depth of 46 metres, on his last attempt in 1967, 106 metres.

Cousteau's efforts were surpassed by a German cave explorer, Jochen Hasenmayer, who reached a depth of 205 metres in 1983. Finally, in 1985, a remote-controlled diving robot went to the bottom depth of 308 metres.

The spring basin is a kind of outsized syphon with a catchment area that stretches from Mont Ventoux to the Montagne de Lure. Visitors to Fontaine-de-Vaucluse in summer will be disappointed, because at this time of year the view is of a boring, opaque waterhole that looks like a cistern. But in the spring when the snow melts, the Sorgue pours down the valley, a wild and raging torrent. When the basin is full, up to 100,000 litres of water per second flow out. It is the world's fifth-largest spring! Fortunately the Sorgue does not dry up in the summer months, as it is fed by underground channels. As clear as crystal, it winds through the town like a green ribbon. Those who enjoy a canoe trip can then paddle all the way to the L'Isle-sur-la-Sorgue.

Address 84800 Fontaine-de-Vaucluse | Directions From L'Isle-sur-la-Sorgue via the D 25; the car parks and the spring are well signposted. There are several car parks in the town. | Tip Not far from the spring in the Chemin du Gouffre, the Ecomusée du Gouffre is open daily in July and August, in other months from Wednesday to Sunday. It has a reconstruction of the world of the caves and information about the famous spring.

36_ The Aqueduc de Barbegal
Water for the mills

While almost every schoolchild has heard of the Pont du Gard, the Aqueduc de Barbegal is only known to ancient historians and experts on Provence. This aqueduct at the southern border of the Alpilles is not a Unesco World Heritage site. This means that visitors who find their way here largely have the place to themselves, as the Aqueduc de Barbegal is completely outside the itineraries of the tourist buses.

It was probably built a few decades later than the Pont du Gard, in order to supply water to Arles. The water was brought from the south slopes of the Alpilles in an artificial channel, and to accomplish this, the aqueduct had to pass through rocks and across a 325-metre-long hollow now known as the Vallon des Arcs. The precision with which the Roman engineers constructed an aqueduct despite using only the simple measuring equipment that was available to them, makes it impossible to disagree with the statement of Pliny the Elder that there is "nothing more wonderful than the supply of water to Rome" in all the world. In later times, Roman architecture was less appreciated, and a road was even built through the middle of the aqueduct.

Behind a hill adjoining it to the south lie the ruins of a mill erected by the Romans. Called the "Meunerie de Barbegal," it is the biggest and best-preserved example of a vertical mill dating from the period of late antiquity.

Sixteen millstones were originally arranged in two rows on sloping terrain. They had a daily capacity of up to 4.5 tons, and could therefore grind enough flour to meet the basic needs of the city of Arles.

The mills were in operation until the early 4th century, after which the site began to decay, as did the aqueduct. Its dilapidated masonry was then overgrown by plants and shrubs.

Address 13990 Fontvieille | Directions Four kilometres south of Fontvieille, directly on the D 82. | Tip About five kilometres southwest lie the impressive ruins of the Abbaye de Montmajour, once one of the richest monasteries in Provence.

37__Daudet's Mill
A fictional writer's den

There are many mills in Provence. But there is only one to which fans of literature come from all around the world. High above Fontvieille, the famous Moulin de Daudet stands on a limestone plateau that is counted as part of the foothills of the Alpilles.

Alphonse Daudet (1840–97) is one of the most popular French authors today. His literary fame is above all due to the success of Tartarin de Tarascon – a merry provincial tale that mainly owes its humour to Provençal local colour – and his fictional book of stories, Letters from My Windmill. Although the windmill, which was built in 1814 and continued to grind wheat until 1915, can be visited in Fontvieille, it is purely a tourist attraction, complemented with a small museum commemorating the writer, including first editions of his works.

Daudet's books were not actually written in Provence but in his attic in Paris. His favourite subject was the differences in mentality between the people of northern and southern France, which he was able to stage in a virtuoso manner. Born in Nîmes, the writer was well acquainted with the peculiarities of his fellow countrymen, as he left home at the age of just 17 to seek his fortune in Paris.

His relationship to Provence remained close, however. In Fontvieille he was a welcome guest in the home of the Ambroy family, who lived on the edge of the village in the Château de Montauban. His experiences there were a constant source of inspiration for Daudet. His books revolve around typical characters from the south of France, vain and boastful, who get through life with peasant cunning.

Daudet was less concerned with a serious exploration of the southern French mentality than with directing his books towards the amusement of readers in Paris and conforming to their ideas of "the simple life" in the Midi.

Address 13990 Fontvieille | Directions The well-signposted Moulin de Daudet is three kilometres south of Fontvieille. | Opening times June–Sept 9am–6pm, Oct–May 10am–noon and 2–5pm | Tip A gentle circular walk leads from the Office de Tourisme along Avenue des Moulins to Daudet's mill, passing two further mills (Moulin Ramet and Moulin Tissot) on the way.

38 Europe's Largest Cedar Forest

A forester's vision

A cedar forest in Provence? At first this may seem like a surprising idea, as the trees that visitors expect to see here are primarily planes, holm oaks and olive trees. Yet this is not a joke: high up on the Petit Luberon is the largest cedar forest in Europe!

As is so often the case, it started with a vision. An energetic forester, who was convinced of the economic benefits of cedar wood, wanted to prove that the North African cedar (Cedrus atlantica) could adapt to the climate of Provence. In 1861 he began to plant imported seeds on the gently rolling terrain of the Luberon. He did not live to see the success of his project, as the woods grew very slowly at first. Even by 1930 the area on which the cedars were growing was no larger than 60 hectares. Today, however, it covers a surface of 250 hectares, and the largest trees have now attained heights of up to 60 metres. The oldest specimens can be recognised by their scaly, slightly cracked and almost black-grey bark.

The cedar forest (Forêt des Cèdres), which is situated between the communes of Lacoste, Bonnieux and Ménerbes, are part of the Parc naturel régional du Luberon, and can be explored on marked walking trails. The ecosystem of these woods, and the flora and fauna of the Petit Luberon area in general, are explained on several information panels along a four-kilometre-long nature trail (sentier botanique). Here you can learn that the North African cedar does not flower until it has reached the age of 25 or 30 years, and that the quickly germinating seeds have a length of more than one centimetre.

From the viewpoint at Les Portalas there is a wonderful, far-ranging view across the broad valley of the Durance as far as the Montagne Sainte-Victoire (see panorama board).

Address Forêt des Cèdres | **Directions** The cedar forest is easily reached from a walkers' car park at the end of a road that branches off from the D 943 1.5 kilometres south of Bonnieux. | Tip Close to the cedar forest, on the road from Ménerbes to Lacoste, lies the Abbaye Saint-Hilaire, a Carmelite monastery founded in 1254. It is now private property but can be visited daily from 10am until 7pm, in winter until 5pm.

39 __ The Industrial Town
Pipelines and storage tanks

Fos-sur-Mer was settled in antiquity and possesses a pretty little old quarter, above which a massive ruined castle rises. Despite this, the sights of Fos-sur-Mer are not described in any guidebook. If you now think that it must be one of the last insiders' tips in Provence, you would be well wide of the mark. On the contrary: most travellers avoid a stop in Fos-sur-Mer and press ahead as fast as they can towards Arles or Marseille.

This is because the town is a warning and a monument to the way in which the belief in progress can ruthlessly destroy a fragile ecosystem. In the 1960s the French government planned to build a new industrial area in the delta of the Rhône. The Gulf of Fos with its deep water seemed ideally suited as a site for heavy industry. Furthermore, this region at the end of the Crau plain was barren and thinly populated, which meant that no great resistance from the locals was expected.

A gigantic industrial landscape with huge dock facilities was designed on the drawing board. The intention was to create more than 150,000 new jobs within two decades. In addition, infrastructure with shopping centres, hospitals, schools and housing for up to 500,000 people was to be built.

The companies that were established here were mainly engaged in processing crude oil. One of them was the Fos oil refinery. However, only ten years later the region felt the effects of the oil crisis of the 1970s, and the scale of "Operation Fos" quickly proved to be too large, causing many projects to be abandoned.

Though 15,000 people live in Fos, its appearance is still dominated by steelworks, cylindrical storage tanks, refinery plants with flaming chimneys, and pipelines. The industrial installations overshadow everything around them, and the natural environment has largely been destroyed.

Address 13270 Fos-sur-Mer | Directions Fos-sur-Mer lies between Arles and Marseille on the N 568. | Tip The 11th-century church of Saint-Sauveur is the most important cultural sight in the town.

40__The Sculpture Garden
Modern art in a famous wine village

Gigondas is known primarily as the origin of great Provençal wines. It may not be quite as famous as Châteauneuf-du-Pape, but its dark red wines, mostly made from Grenache grapes, are among the best in France.

So it is not surprising that most visitors to this little town at the foot of the Dentelles de Montmirail come to buy or to sample wine. It is hard to overlook the numerous signs advertising a dégustation. After a tasting, people take a stroll through the village before sitting down at a table shaded by plane trees in one of the restaurants, L'Oustalet or Du Verre à l'Assiette. There's no doubt about it – this is a wonderful way to pass a few hours.

Unfortunately almost all visitors leave out the pleasant walk through the modern sculpture garden, which was laid out in 1994 on the initiative of the society Gigondas d'Hier et d'Aujourd'hui in the ruins of an old hospice above the medieval village. It only takes a few minutes to walk there.

A few dozen sculptures by contemporary French and international artists are on display. Works of art made from wood, metal and stone are scattered over an extensive site that has an atmospheric setting amongst ancient walls.

Just as every vintage is different from the last one for the winemakers of Gigondas, each year the sculpture garden changes its appearance.

In November it gets its annual "makeover" with new works of art. In a small room devoted to exhibitions, visitors can learn about the history and the restoration of the hospice through a display of photographs, and also find information about more than 100 artists and over 300 sculptures that have so far been put on show in Gigondas. The idea of combining enjoyment of art with a wine tasting is both inspiring and stimulating!

Address 84190 Gigondas | Directions From Orange head east on the D23 and D7. | Opening times Wed–Sun Nov–March 2–5pm, April, May 11am–12.30pm and 2–6pm, June, Sept and Oct 2–6pm; July, Aug daily 10.30am–12.30pm and 2.30–6.30pm | Tip On the first Sunday in June a festival with music and the exhibiting artists is held.

41 Gorges de la Méouge
Motorbikes and waterfalls

The canyon landscapes of the south of France have a magical attraction for bikers. There is hardly a rocky valley bottom in all of Provence where motorcyclists don't tilt coolly into the curves. In the Gorges de la Méouge, too, you can hardly avoid them, even though this little canyon in Haute-Provence is off the beaten track for tourists. If you want to avoid motor traffic, you have to opt for the walking trail that passes along the right bank.

The Méouge – the name "Méoujo" in the Provençal language means "honey-coloured water" – is a comparatively small river. It flows for a distance of almost 40 kilometres across shimmering red rock from its source to its confluence with the Buëch. In the course of thousands of years, the Méouge has carved out a wonderful riverbed with many waterfalls and rock pools – inviting spots for swimming and cooling off.

In spring, when the snow melts and water pours into the valley from the surrounding mountains, kayakers take advantage of the floodwater to paddle through the rocky gorge. In summer the Gorges de la Méouge are the domain of hikers and people looking for a place to swim.

The few places to park a car in the narrow valley are quickly taken on holiday weekends, as the locals from nearby Sisteron like to come here for a refreshing dip in the pools. Despite its popularity, there is enough space for everyone on the banks of the river – somewhere or other it is always possible to find a rock where you can doze in the sun.

A hint for swimmers: the best place is close to a conspicuous three-arched "Roman bridge", which actually dates from the late Middle Ages. Close to this bridge, those who are daring to jump into the milky turquoise waters from a height of almost ten metres. The bridge spans the river near the middle of the gorge.

Address Georges de la Méouge | Directions The D 942 passes along the whole length of the Gorges de la Méouge, which lies 20 kilometres north-west of Sisteron. | Tip It is worth taking the short trip to the picture-postcard Mison Village. A little dead-end road winds up to the village, where the houses cluster around a castle.

42 Gorges du Régalon
The narrowest canyon in Provence

Among the many canyons in Provence, the Gorges du Régalon can claim a special distinction: they are the narrowest in the region! At their most confined point, where walls of rock rise to a height of 40 metres, you can almost touch both sides of the gorge at once with your shoulders!

The path that leads to the canyons is pretty. From the walkers' car park you pass through a small olive grove with benches for picnics before reaching a dried-out riverbed. From here the path becomes stonier and more uneven; then come the first ascents. It is not necessary to have a knowledge of climbing, but sturdy shoes with a good tread on the sole are advisable rather than flip-flops, as the stones can be extremely slippery, especially after rain! For children it is a real adventure to explore the canyon, which was created around six million years ago, as you have to clamber over blocks of stone in a number of places. In one especially spectacular spot the trail passes through a cave tunnel – so take a flashlight with you – and in other places the path is so narrow that you can only walk single file and have to stop and move aside when hikers approach from the opposite direction.

A few chunks of rock have tumbled into the gorge and look somewhat threatening, as they have become wedged between the close-standing rock walls. A few years ago the canyon was even closed for months following a rock fall. The caves to the left and right were inhabited in the Stone Age. Hunters and gatherers found a refuge and shelter here.

After about an hour you reach the end of the dark gorge and see a small shady wood with box trees, privet and many small-leaved deciduous trees – a refreshing sight! From here you can either return by the same route or walk westwards across the plateau and go back to the starting point through Vallon de la Roque Rousse.

Address 84460 Cheval-Blanc | Directions The Gorges du Régalon are eleven kilometres east of Cavaillon. Near the D 973 a car park for walkers (charges apply) is signposted near La Tuillère. | Tip For the walk over the plateau, the IGN walkers map no. 3142 OT, scale 1:25.000, is useful. It can be bought in every Maison de la Presse within 50 kilometres.

43__ The Grand Canyon du Verdon

252 steps between heaven and earth

Go up or go down – this is the decision at the start of every hiking trip through the Grand Canyon du Verdon. At the heart of the walking trail there is an awe-inspiring section called Sentier Martel, where a rusty iron ladder is wedged between steep rocks with steps that are often slippery after rain. Depending on whether you prefer to climb up or down the 252 steps, you start the tour in La Maline or at Point Sublime.

It is usually easier to go up, so most walkers begin their exploration of the most spectacular canyon in the south of France at Point Sublime.

Until 1905 the Grand Canyon du Verdon was regarded as unconquerable. In that year the French caver Édouard Alfred Martel, in the company of local guides, succeeded in passing through the canyon for the very first time on a three-day expedition. On the trail that bears Martel's name you can walk through the key section of the canyon in about six hours.

This is an adventurous undertaking even apart from the iron ladder: the very first steps make an unforgettable impression, as you walk on limestone rock only a few metres above the emerald-green water. The path then leads above the abyss along overhanging walls of rock. Later you pass through a tunnel that is almost 700 metres long and as dark as night. The beam of your flashlight illuminates small puddles, and light is admitted through a narrow gap in the rock only in one place. To cap it all, you have to traverse a rubble-covered slope with the assistance of wire cables.

All these efforts are rewarded by magnificent views of a canyon landscape, scenery that was untouched by civilisation for a very long time.

Address Gorges du Verdon | **Directions** The Grand Canyon du Verdon is in the northeast of Provence. Point Sublime lies on the D 952 between Moustiers-Sainte-Marie and Castellane. | **Tip** To return to the starting point you either have to hitchhike – which usually works well – or call a taxi. There are two taxi services for walkers in the Gorges du Verdon: Trans Verdon Taxi, tel. 0033/0607651949; Taxi Verdon, tel. 0033/0668181313.

44 The Café de la Poste

One deadly summer

The Café de la Poste is an established institution in Goult.

Situated right on the marketplace, it is a place where locals as well as the owners of holiday homes meet to chat over a pastis or a glass of cold beer. You can also order a three-course meal here or buy a newspaper, as Café de la Poste is an unusual mixture of café, restaurant and newsagent; its furnishings have hardly changed in decades.

This café has cult status – not only for locals but also for cinema fans. In 1982 its counter was the set for a few scenes in the film "One Deadly Summer," in which the young Isabelle Adjani made a tempestuous comeback after taking a break from acting to have a baby. In this film Adjani sealed her reputation as one of Europe's most popular actresses, and was awarded a César in the category of best actress for the role in 1984.

In "One Deadly Summer" she plays the part of Eliane, a young femme fatale who is searching for three men who once raped her mother. She appears as if out of nowhere in a provincial town in the south of France that is gasping in the summer heat, and turns the heads of all the men in the village with her provocative clothing and saucy manner. The somewhat simple-minded car mechanic Pin Pon falls in love with Eliane, but ultimately she only uses him to reveal the dark secret of her origins. When she comes to the conclusion that she has identified two of the guilty men as the owner of the sawmill Leballech and the estate agent Touret, a fateful catastrophe runs its course …

"One Deadly Summer" is regarded to this day as Isabelle Adjani's most popular film. With her impulsive and libidinous portrayal of Eliane she captivated audiences everywhere. The film's locations, in addition to Goult, were the villages of Lioux and Villars, as well as Carpentras.

Address Rue de la République, 84220 Goult, tel. 0033/0490722323 | Directions Goult lies between Cavaillon and Apt, a little to the north of the N 110. Rue de la République is in the town centre. | Opening times Wed–Tue 8am–11pm | Tip In Goult don't miss the walk to the upper part of the village to see the remains of a castle.

45 — The Templar Castle
The legend lives on

Gréoux-les-Bains is a lively little spa with thermal baths that has a long tradition. The Romans are said to have alleviated their rheumatism and arthritis in the warm Griselis spring, and the famous Provençal poet Jean Giono, who lived in the neighbouring Manosque, was aware of a further healing effect, saying that he knew "no place that heals discontent better than Gréoux."

The springs and thermal baths are on the eastern edge of the little town, which is crowned by the ruins of a castle of the Knights Templar. Although it is always spoken of as a "Château des Templiers," in fact this fortress dating from the 12th century was not built by the powerful Order of the Temple but originally belonged to the counts of Provence and later passed into the ownership of the Order of the Knights of St John of Malta (Hospitaliers de St Jean de Jérusalem).

Nevertheless, the legend that the Templars built the castle in order to use the healing properties of the water to cure wounded knights has taken root as firmly as the assertion that there is a secret passage leading underground from a cistern into the castle. Those who are interested in the Templars can follow in their footsteps in several places in Provence, for example in Richerenches or Marseille, but not here.

In summer open-air performances are staged in the rectangular castle courtyard. Over the centuries the fortress has been extended and reinforced several times. Like so many French palaces and castles, the "Château des Templiers" suffered in the upheavals of the Revolution. It was stormed and set afire, so that today only impressive ruins rise above the spa town.

The castle's keep and other towers can still be clearly identified, however. The best-preserved part is the former guardhouse, which is used for exhibitions.

Address 04800 Gréoux-les-Bains | Directions Take the A 51 to the exit for Manosque, then continue east, first on the D 4, then on the D 82 to the town centre, where you can't miss the castle. | Tip The thermal baths in Avenue des Thermes are open from March to September. Various thermal treatments are on offer; www.chainethermale.fr.

46 The Monument to Madame de Sévigné

1500 letters from Paris to Province

On a small square beneath the château of Grignan a monument for Marie de Rabutin-Chantal, better known as Madame de Sévigné (1626–96), was erected in 1857. Rightly so, as thanks to her Grignan has found a place in literary history.

Marie, praised for her beauty and high standard of education by all her contemporaries, kept a well-regarded salon in Paris and moved in the best circles. As her husband had died young, she had a very close relationship with her only daughter, Françoise-Marguerite. When the husband of Françoise-Marguerite, the Comte de Grignan, was appointed deputy governor of Provence and Françoise had to leave Paris with him, Madame de Sévigné was extremely downcast and experienced great longing for her daughter. Nevertheless, the close mother-daughter relationship lasted a lifetime.

There survive almost 1500 letters in which Madame de Sévigné sent detailed descriptions of everyday matters and the social life of the French aristocracy in the age of Louis XIV to her daughter in Provence. In her lively chronicle, which is among the literary classics of the 17th century, she also sang the praises of the abundant and excellent food in Provence, which she had come to know and love on her visits there: "The white figs are as sweet as sugar, the grapes like edible balls of amber. It would be easy to get intoxicated on them." On the other hand she left no doubt about the fact that she thought the provincial south of France a godforsaken place ("Oh, the smell!").

During her third stay with her daughter in Grignan, Madame de Sévigné fell ill and died after ten days on her sickbed. Her letters, a fascinating testimony to an age of magnificence, are remembered to this day. On the monument she was therefore portrayed in a pensive pose, engaged in writing a letter.

Marie
de Rabutin - Chantal
marquise de Sévigné.

Address Place Sévigné, 26230 Grignan | **Directions** Via the A7, exit to Montélimar Sud, then 17 kilometres east on the D541. The monument is in the centre of Grignan. | **Tip** The imposing Renaissance château of Grignan with its wonderful panorama terrace can be visited daily on a guided tour between 9.30am and noon or from 2pm until 6pm.

47__Villa Noailles
Cubist ocean liner

To look upon Villa Noailles, high above the old quarter of Hyères, you might think that a Cubist-style ocean liner had run aground. But appearances are deceptive: it is not a ship that has anchored at the edge of Parc Saint-Bernard, but a 40-room villa. Commissioned in 1924 by Vicomte Charles de Noailles and his wife Marie-Laure, the architect Robert Mallet-Stevens built a winter residence with an indoor pool, gym and squash court that is clearly inspired by Cubism. The task of designing the interior was entrusted to Marcel Breuer and Pierre Chareau, who chose to use furniture by Eileen Gray.

The garden, too, with a triangular shape reminiscent of the bow of a ship, is a fascinating feature. Squares and rectangles clad with red, blue, purple, black, yellow and grey ceramic tiles form a chequerboard pattern at its centre.

As the wealthy Vicomte de Noailles had avant-garde leanings and saw himself as a patron of the arts, he often invited well-known artists to live and work in the luxurious guest suites of his residence. For a time Giacometti formed his sculptures in the garden of the villa, and the photographer Man Ray made one of his few films here ("Les Mystères du Château du Dé"). A frequent guest was the director Luis Buñuel, whose scandalous film "L'Age d'Or" was financed by Charles de Noailles.

Since 1973 the estate has been owned by the municipality of Hyères, which uses the rooms for rotating exhibitions and has also installed a permanent exhibition about the couple who built the house. The garden with its geometric shapes is accessible at all times. Villa Noailles is also known for a renowned fashion and photography festival, held annually in late April. Up-and-coming young designers present their work to a high-calibre jury, which has included Christian Lacroix, John Galliano and Yohji Yamamoto.

Address Montée de Noailles, 83400 Hyères, www.villanoailles-hyeres.com | Directions
From Toulon take the A570 eastwards to the end of the motorway. Villa Noailles lies above
the town and is reached via Avenue Paul Long. | Opening times Oct–June Wed–Sun
10am–12.30pm and 2–5.30pm, July–Sept Wed, Thu, Sat–Mon 10am–12.30pm and
2–7pm, Fri 4–10pm | Tip Parc Saint-Bernard with its magnolias, gnarled olive trees and
agave plants is a pleasant place for a walk.

48__The Lac de Sainte-Croix
A reservoir with a history

France is seen as the country that promotes nuclear power, but critics of this policy often overlook the fact that it is also a pioneer in the field of hydroelectric energy. In the southeast of the country there is hardly a single river that does not generate power by means of a few turbines as it flows towards the sea.

The Lac de Sainte-Croix – the second-largest reservoir in France – owes its existence to the French demand for electricity. Between 1971 and 1973 an arch-shaped dam, 95 metres high and 133 metres long, was built to hold back the waters of the Verdon; then began the flooding of 2200 hectares of land to create the lake. As such decisions are made by a centralised government in France, no notice was taken of the protests of local residents whose properties were forcibly appropriated and whose livelihoods as farmers were erased in a flash: beneath the waters, which are up to 50 metres deep, lie not only two villages but also a supposedly "Roman" bridge with nine arches on which the Verdon could be crossed near Aiguines for a period of almost 1500 years. Regrettably there was no interest at that time in moving this historic structure and reinstalling it in another place.

Today faceless modern buildings characterise the scene in Les Salles-sur-Verdon. Of the old village, only the bell from the church tower, the fountain, and the war memorial have been preserved; the rest was blown up and consigned to the floods.

A side effect of this was the emergence of a tourist infrastructure, including campsites, boat rentals and surf centres, without which this economically troubled region could hardly survive. The lake, with water that appears turquoise or emerald green, depending on the light, has a good deal to offer: with water temperatures well over 20°C in summer, it is extremely suitable for all kinds of water sports.

Address Lac de Sainte-Croix | **Directions** The Lac de Sainte-Croix lies between the Plateau de Valensole and the Gorges du Verdon. Apart from two places, where the roads pass through its hinterland, it is possible to drive round the lake close to the shore. | Tip At several places pedaloes can be hired. To get an impression of life in Les Salles-sur-Verdon before the village was flooded, see the information and photos at www.lessallessurverdon.com/LSenv.html.

49__ The Boule Ground
Feet together

Many pioneering inventions are born in response to a shortcoming. One example of this is the famous Provençal game of pétanque, which is often falsely described in other countries as boule. The favourite sport of the people of Provence, which was praised by the writer and film director Marcel Pagnol as "the most beautiful game ever invented by man," was first devised in 1907 on the beach promenade at La Ciotat.

The businessman Jules Hugues, known as "Le Noir" ("the Black One"), was a passionate boule player. As an old man he suffered so badly from rheumatism that he was no longer able to play his beloved game, which involved throwing a ball some 20 metres after taking a running start. He sat around unhappily in Ernest and Joseph Pitiot's bar, until he and the brothers jointly came up with the idea of trying out a shorter version of the game, in which the balls were thrown from a standing position without a run-up, in the open space in front of the bar.

Pétanque was colossally successful. The name is derived from "pieds tanqués" ("standing with feet together"). In no time at all the game spread across all of Provence and almost completely replaced the old pastime of boule, which was also known as "longue" or "jeu provençal." As early as 1910 the first official pétanque competition was held in La Ciotat.

The new sport owed its widespread popularity to its relatively simple rules and the fact that you can play pétanque on almost any kind of surface. Two teams, with two or three persons per side and three balls each, compete against one another. The aim is to throw the iron balls, which weigh almost 900 grams, as close as possible to a small wooden ball called the "cochonnet" ("piglet"), which lies at a distance of between six and ten metres. The first team to reach 13 points wins the match.

Address Boulevard Georges Clemenceau, 13600 La Ciotat | Directions From Marseille via the A 50, exit for La Ciotat, then towards the Office de Tourisme. | Tip To find out more about the history or rules of boule/pétanque, or to order balls, go to www.laboulebleue.fr.

50__Calanque de Figuerolles
An independent bay like paradise

The year is 2014. The whole of Provence has been occupied by the French … the whole of Provence? No! One small bay continues to hold out against the invaders …

This last bastion of resistance is the République Indépendante de Figuerolles (R. I. F. for short), a small cove framed by steeply rising rock walls that looks almost like paradise, where Georges Braque once set up his painter's easel in 1909.

In keeping with its status as an independent "republic" the R. I. F. not only has its own "border," which runs next to the car park, but also its own traffic regulations (keep left on the steps!), its own currency and its own time zone, one hour behind the time in neighbouring France … oh yes, and the clocks in the Calanque de Figuerolles run slower, as its current "president," Grégori Reverchon, has proudly announced.

The R. I. F. was established back in 1956 by Grégori's grandparents, Igor and Tania, who came from Russia. In the bay they founded a little café called Chez Tania. Since 1994 their grandson has taken the "family bay" – which, by the way, is freely accessible for anyone who wants to swim or sunbathe there – into his loving care and has carefully turned the simple café into a small hotel and restaurant without spoiling the unconventional charm of the spot.

Visitors once simply slept beneath the fig trees. Now there are three basic but clean rooms, each with a shower and a terrace, as well as four bungalows grouped around an idyllic garden. The colourful restaurant with its thatched patio nestled in the cliffs offers a magnificent view across the bay. The menu features appealing Mediterranean cuisine with an Asian touch. Whether you order grilled bream or perch – the fish has been freshly caught! Customers who put in their order 48 hours in advance can also enjoy a typical Marseille bouillabaisse.

Address Avenue Figuerolles, 13600 La Ciotat. Restaurant: tel. 0033/0442084171, www.figuerolles.com | Directions From Marseille take the A50, exit to La Ciotat. The Calanque de Figuerolles is about one kilometre southwest of the harbour. There are a couple dozen free parking spaces above the bay. | Tip From the Calanque de Figuerolles a walking trail leads along the Corniche des Crêtes to Cassis.

51 Cinema Lumière de l'Eden
The Provençal Hollywood

When most people think of the cradle of cinema, Hollywood, New York, or perhaps even Paris come to mind. Yet the earliest cinema history was not made in America, but in a French province. The first film location in the history of movies was the train station at La Ciotat.

During their stay here in summer 1895, Auguste and Louis Lumière, two pioneers of film who came from a wealthy family in Lyon, placed a newly developed camera apparatus next to the tracks and filmed the arrival of a train.

The first screening in the Grand Café on Boulevard des Capucines in Paris led to uproar and terror among the spectators: in the film ("L'Arrivée d'un train en gare de La Ciotat"), which lasted less than a minute, the audience was skilfully given the impression that the train was rushing straight at them. The effect of this unknown medium was enormous, and the global triumph of "moving pictures" began.

In their passion for cinema, the Lumière brothers made further short films in La Ciotat, including the first-ever staged comedy in movie history – about a gardener who accidentally waters himself ("L'Arroseur arose"). They also screened their works in the town at the Eden-Théâtre. This unimpressive theatre, situated a few hundred metres east of the old harbour, was built in 1889 for performing plays and concerts, as well as for boxing and wrestling matches. Today the Eden-Théâtre is a protected monument, and is regarded as "the oldest cinema in the world." Following a long period in which it was no longer used as a cinema, the decision has recently been made to restore it.

In La Ciotat there is another cinema. It bears the name "Lumière" after the founding fathers of the medium, and is adorned with an oversized double portrait of the brothers.

Address 25, Boulevard Georges Clemenceau, 13600 La Ciotat, www.leslumieresdeleden.fr | Directions From Marseille take the A 50, exit to La Ciotat, then head for the Office de Tourisme. | Tip A boat trip to Île Verte is pleasant. This small island off La Ciotat has two attractive beaches, and boats go out every half hour in summer.

52 The Shipyards
Where ocean giants were forged

In contrast to the neighbouring coastal towns of Cassis and Bandol, La Ciotat can point to a great history as the home of shipyards and industry. When you stand on the hills above the town or look out to sea from the terrace of a street café on the old harbour, you cannot fail to see the gigantic cranes used for shipbuilding and carrying loads. In its heyday, between the 16th and the 18th century, La Ciotat was even a rival for the commercial port of Marseille. Later, however, the town concentrated on the business of shipbuilding.

For a long time the local shipyards ensured that the inhabitants of La Ciotat could make a steady living. La Ciotat was the only French port on the Mediterranean that possessed docks where ships of more than 500,000 tons could be constructed. Huge freight and passenger ships were built in the Chantiers Navals de la Ciotat. One of them, the tanker Al Rawdatain, even had a length of more than 350 metres! This glorious past also had its darker side: directly by the harbour pier a monument erected in 2007 commemorates the numerous workers who lost their lives or whose health was damaged by the use of asbestos in shipbuilding.

Rails in the asphalt are a reminder that the employees used to go to work by tram. At their peak, the shipyards employed well over 5000 people. La Ciotat was a typical workers' town, which was ruled between 1977 and 2001 by three mayors of the Communist Party (PCF).

For more than three decades now La Ciotat has been struggling with economic and social problems caused by the international crisis in the shipbuilding industry – it is not only cities like Glasgow, Newcastle-upon-Tyne and Bremen that have suffered from the competition of Asian countries with low labour costs. So the shipyards of La Ciotat reconsidered their business model, and now mainly concentrate on making and repairing luxury yachts.

Address 13600 La Ciotat, www.laciotat-shipyards.com | Directions From Marseille take the A 50, exit to La Ciotat, then head for the Office de Tourisme. | Tip The Musée Ciotaden on Quai Ganteaume gives thorough attention to the shipbuilding tradition of La Ciotat. It is open daily except Tuesday from June to September from 4pm to 7pm, and from October to May from 3pm to 6pm.

53___The Tip of the Church Tower

A bell cage for the mistral

The mistral should not be taken lightly. This cold downslope wind that comes along the Rhône valley is the true ruler of Provence, and even large trees bend in deference to its power. With top speeds of well over 100 kilometres per hour it blows south without ever stopping for breath. It once kept people imprisoned in their homes for days at a time during the winter, nagging at their nerves with its whining and whistling. An old farmers' adage says: "The mistral that rose before first light goes back to bed the following night; the mistral that starts up after dawn takes three, six or nine days before it's done."

The mistral has had a decisive influence on the region's architecture. Almost without exception, Provençal houses turn their windowless side to the wind, and slate-covered roofs are not permitted on church towers or the towers of city gates. This is why bells ring out from an artistically forged cage open to the sky, as this construction gives the wind only a small surface to attack. In Provence there are altogether about 250 of these iron cages, called "campaniles," usually holding small bells. A particularly beautiful, though unusual example adorns the beffroi of Lacoste. Borne on three round stone columns, this little masterpiece of wrought iron arches beneath the sky.

The people of Provence owe not only their bell cages to the mistral but also their superb clear blue skies, because it sweeps away all the clouds. Artists such as Vincent van Gogh were fascinated by this spectacle: "When the mistral is blowing, this is anything but a 'mild country,' as the mistral is a great irritation. But how great is the compensation when a calm day comes! What radiance of colour, what pure air, what tranquil lightness of spirit."

Address 84480 Lacoste | Directions Lacoste is on the northern edge of the Luberon, four kilometres south of the N100, which links Avignon with Apt. | Tip Beneath the village the Café de France has a terrace with a wonderful view across to Bonnieux.

54 Marquis de Sade Monument

Commemoration of a sadistic free-thinker

Lacoste is not merely the brand name of a well-known polo shirt with a crocodile logo, but also a pretty little village on the northern edge of the Luberon mountains whose claim to fame is being the ancestral home of the family of the infamous Marquis de Sade (1740–1814).

High above the village stand the ruins of the chateau of the de Sade family, which was looted during the French Revolution. Today the Château de Lacoste is owned by the fashion designer Pierre Cardin – a fact that the locals greet with little enthusiasm. Although the designer has initiated urgently needed renovation work and organised exhibitions and concerts, he's also ruthlessly been buying up deserted and dilapidated buildings to the point that he now possesses almost half of the village.

Next to the chateau, on permanent loan as it were, stands a statue of the Marquis de Sade by the Russian artist Alexandre Bourganov: it shows the head of the marquis enclosed in a cage, above oversized folded arms.

Who was the notorious marquis, who had to spend a third of his life behind bars? He was primarily a free-thinker and committed atheist, who was moved by the spirit of the Enlightenment and spoke out clearly against the death penalty. However, the Marquis de Sade became famous above all for his sexual obsessions, which he regarded as "immutable" and "incurable." The prostitutes of Marseille, whom he treated with extreme roughness, took a critical view of this, by contrast. He coped with the hardships of imprisonment with the help of his erotic writings, but their publication brought him another spell behind bars. Whether incest or sodomy – de Sade felt bound by no taboos: "It is not my way of thinking that has brought misfortune upon me, but the way that others think."

Address Place du Château, 84480 Lacoste | **Directions** Lacoste is on the northern edge of the Luberon, four kilometres south of the N 100, which links Avignon with Apt. The monument is above the village next to the ruined castle. | **Tip** On the road from Lacoste to Ménerbes a signposted track branches off left after some two kilometres and leads a short distance to the abbey of Saint-Hilaire, founded in 1254.

55 The Grottes de Calès
Living room of the aboriginal Provençals

Lamanon is both pleasant and unexciting. It has everything needed to make a lively village, but apart from a single small chateau it possesses no outstanding sights. Nevertheless, there is one good reason to visit this place in the département of Bouches-du-Rhône: the Grottes de Calès, situated above Lamanon, are one of the largest and most significant prehistoric complexes of cave dwellings in France.

From the church it only takes a few minutes to go up the mountain to the stone gate of Cirque de Calès. The caves, which lie beyond in a kind of elevated valley, were probably already inhabited in the Neolithic period. It is thought that they may once have been occupied by as many as 150 families.

The simple dwellings and spacious storerooms were hewn out of the soft limestone of the Alpilles. In some places this created a strange sequence of rooms, including steps, arched gates and windows. Archaeological studies estimate that almost 60 inhabited caves were occupied all year round in the rock bowl. A sophisticated system of channels, also carved out of the rock, fed cisterns that supplied the cave population with water. Excavations have uncovered pottery, bones, and the remains of grain – providing insights into the diet of people in those times.

Because they were situated in a place that was easy to defend, the caves were not only used as dwellings for the Ligurians but also as a safe shelter in the early Middle Ages in the event of Saracen raids. The last people who holed up in the caves were refugees during the French Wars of Religion. After the end of the Huguenot wars, the caves were abandoned for good.

It is an enjoyable activity, especially for children, to explore the hidden chambers and the freely accessible caves, and to imagine the simple life that early settlers led here in the Stone Age.

Address 13113 Lamanon | **Directions** Lamanon is on the N538, seven kilometres north of Salon-de-Provence. | **Tip** In Lamanon a small museum presents the finds from Calès. It is open on the first and third Sunday of each month; www.cales-lamanon.fr.

56__La Treille
In the footsteps of Marcel Pagnol

The writer and film director Marcel Pagnol, a member of the famous Académie Française, is one of the most popular Provençal authors to this day. His novels Marius, Fanny, and La Gloire de Mon Père (My Father's Glory), are still widely read. All around the hamlet of La Treille, beneath Mont Garlaban, you can follow in the footsteps of Pagnol.

Marcel Pagnol was born in 1895 in nearby Aubagne and grew up in Marseille, where his father was a primary-school teacher. From his childhood onwards he was closely attached to La Treille, as the family possessed a holiday home there. He described the summer of 1904, when the Pagnols spent their holidays in the "Bastide Neuve" (which still exists, one kilometre north of the village) for the first time, as the happiest time of his life: "The air was still, and the spicy scent of the hills filled the gorge like an invisible mist. Thyme, lavender and rosemary mingle with the smell of the golden-yellow resin, whose long, immobile tears gleamed like glass on the light shadows of the black bark of the trees. I marched silently in the tranquillity of this solitude."

The events of those days form the principal narrative strand in his novel, La Gloire de Mon Père. With his friend Lili, Pagnol roams around the hills and valleys beneath the 714-metre-high Mont Garlaban and carries the reader away with him for innocent adventures in an idyll made of sunshine and lavender.

Today numerous walking trails criss-cross the hilly landscape known as the "Collines de Pagnol." With a little luck you might spot a few bartavelles (rock partridges). Hunting these birds plays an important role in Pagnol's novel. An essential part of a trip to the area is a visit to the village cemetery of La Treille to see the grave of Pagnol, who has rested there, along with members of his family, since 18 April 1974.

Address La Treille, 13013 Marseille | **Directions** From the A 50 turn onto the D 44, then north between Aubagne and Allauch (there are bus connections to Marseille) towards La Treille. | **Tip** The birthplace of Marcel Pagnol at Aubagne 16, Cours Barthélmy, is open to visitors daily in summer, daily except Monday in winter.

57 __ Circuit Paul Ricard

Round and round at record speed

Formula 1 in Provence? The very idea seems a little odd. Yet it is true: Silverstone, the Nürburgring and Monaco are not the only places where high-powered racing cars zoom around a track. Some 30 kilometres from the French Mediterranean coast, there is another venue called the Circuit Paul Ricard.

As the name suggests, the initiative came from the French pastis producer Paul Ricard, who acquired a barren plateau between Toulon and Marseille, building a private airfield there and a racetrack, which was inaugurated in 1970 and quickly became a Mecca for fans of motor sport. From 1971 until 1990 the French Grand Prix was held on the circuit, which is almost six kilometres long. The names of Jackie Stewart and Niki Lauda are included on the list of illustrious winners; the victor in the last Formula 1 race that was held here was Alain Prost.

The motorbike world championships were also held here, as was a classic long-distance motorcycle race, the Bol d'Or, which took place at this track until 1999. The Circuit Paul Ricard has now long been forgotten, even though it is owned by the head of Formula 1, Bernie Ecclestone.

Today the events held on the Circuit Paul Ricard are go-kart races and the finale of the GT Tour. The track is mainly used as a test run by various racing teams, and tyre makers such as Pirelli come here to try out their new rubber materials. Several manufacturers of sports cars also use it to train drivers in special conditions. For prices starting at 30,000 euros, the organisers of private events and motor clubs can rent the whole infrastructure of the track. An extremely popular activity on certain days are test drives for private individuals who always dreamed that one day they would take the wheel of a Ferrari F458 Italia, a Lamborghini Gallardo, a Porsche 997 GT3 RS or an Audi R8 V10.

Address 2760, Route des Hauts du Camp, 83330 Le Castellet, www.circuitpaulricard.com |
Directions The Circuit Paul Ricard lies between Aubagne and Toulon on the N 8 and is
extremely well signposted. | Tip There are two hotels right by the track: the Grand Prix
Hôtel, www.grandprixhotel.fr, and the Hôtel du Castellet, www.hotelducastellet.com.

58 The Best Olive Oil in Provence

A golden-green delicacy

The olive tree, like the vine, is part of the heritage of Greek culture. Pampered by the Mediterranean climate, it flourishes all over Provence, but there are only a few regions where farmers devote themselves entirely to its cultivation. Alongside the olive oil from Nyons in northern Provence, those from the Vallée des Baux have an outstanding reputation.

Beneath the castle of Les Baux, the Alpilles mountain range falls away gently south towards Maussane-les-Alpilles. Here the sun smiles on a wonderful landscape of silver-shimmering olive groves. Gourmets claim that the very best olive oil in France comes from here. It earns plaudits for its velvety texture and notes of dried fruit and almonds.

Since 1997 the olive oils from the Vallée des Baux have possessed an AOC rating that guarantees their authentic origin. Eight mills process the fruit of almost 400,000 trees, which are harvested in November. Following harvesting, the olives are stored at the mill for a period of time, as the slight process of fermentation that then begins allows additional aromas to develop. Between five and eight kilograms of olives are required in order to extract one litre of the best oil in the first cold pressing; this golden-green "huile d'olive vierge" is characterised by an acid content of one percent at most, and sometimes even less.

It goes without saying that the olive oils produced in the Vallée des Baux are not low-cost supermarket oils, but expensive natural products that sell for approximately 20 euros per litre. They are almost too good to be used for cooking. If you decide to buy one, it is best to use it for making a fine salad dressing in summer, or to dip a slice of bread in it, or to drizzle it on a piece of good goat's-milk cheese.

Address 13520 Les Baux | **Directions** Les Baux is on the D 78, about 20 kilometres north-east of Arles. | **Tip** Outstanding olive oil is produced and sold at the Moulin du Mas des Barres in Maussane-les-Alpilles from Monday to Saturday, 9am – 12 noon and 2 – 6.30pm; www.masdesbarres.com.

59__ The Mines of Light

Where dream worlds are staged

Travellers who happen to journey north from Les Baux through the Alpilles can hardly believe their eyes: suddenly they are confronted with huge, gaping square cave entrances, 10 metres high, that look as if a Cyclops had cut them out of the rock with a gigantic knife. These impressive halls are not, however, the relics of a mystic past but a reminder of the extraction of bauxite that once flourished here. The name of the sedimentary rock needed to produce aluminium is, in fact, a reference to the place where it was discovered in 1821, Les Baux.

The almost surreal atmosphere of the abandoned, deeply branching mines inspired Jean Cocteau to make his last film here in 1959. "Testament of Orpheus" is regarded as both the cinematic legacy of Cocteau, and also as a "family film," because many of his friends and long-standing companions, including Jean Marais and Yul Brynner, took roles, and others such as Pablo Picasso followed the work of filming.

The artist Albert Plécy, too, was fascinated by the atmosphere here, and in 1977 decided to transform a disused bauxite mine close to the village into a "cathédrale d'images."

On an area of 4000 square metres, with the help of more than a dozen projectors casting images onto the bare limestone walls, and a sensitive musical background, Plécy created an experience that made you forget time and space. Every year since that first installation, visitors to the "Carrières de Lumières," to use the official name of the event, are taken on a new audio-visual journey, so that there is no chance for boredom. There is a highly diverse range of shows using sound and light. The subjects so far have included "A Winter in Venice," "Michelangelo in the Sistine Chapel," "The Middle Ages of Light" and in 2012, "Gaugin – Van Gogh – Painters of Colour."

Address 13520 Les Baux, www.carrieres-lumieres.com | **Directions** Les Baux is on the D 78 about 20 kilometres northeast of Arles. The mines are a few hundred metres northwest of the village on the D 27. | **Opening times** April–Sept daily 10am–7pm, Oct–March 10am–6pm | **Tip** Don't miss a screening of Cocteau's film "Testament of Orpheus," which is shown in a mine converted to a cinema.

60__ The Pilgrims' Church

The destination of the annual "gypsy pilgrimage"

The Camargue is as flat as a pancake, which means that the crenellated pilgrimage church of Notre-Dame-de-la-Mer, whose appearance is reminiscent of the upturned skeleton of a stranded ship, can be seen from many miles away. The dark, candle-lit crypt of this fortified church, where a statue of St Sarah decorated with jewellery is housed, is the Mecca of the European Roma and Sinti people.

According to a Christian legend, after the death of Christ, a few of his followers, including Mary Magdalene, Mary Jacobe and Mary Salome – the latter two were the mothers of three apostles – were placed in a boat without either sails or oars. Through divine providence they were carried over the sea to the shores of Provence, an event that represented the beginning of Christianity in the Provincia Gallia Narbonensis. The Three Maries have long been overshadowed by their servant Sarah, who is said to have been a gypsy on account of her dark skin.

Each year on 24 and 25 May thousands of Roma and Sinti from all parts of Europe make their way to Les-Saintes-Maries-de-la-Mer. Paying tribute to their patron saint is the religious and social highlight of their year.

Following afternoon Mass, the statue, decorated with gold and brocade, is carried to the sea in a big procession with a great show of devotion, together with the relics of the Three Maries, which are lowered from the chapel above. Several gardiens (guards) ride ahead on white Carmague horses while the pilgrims walk proudly through the streets to an accompaniment of music and prayers. "Vive les Saintes Maries, vive la Sainte Sarah," is the cry that rings out. Slowly the procession approaches the sea, where the saints are symbolically welcomed. The bishop of Arles then blesses the sea, the land, the pilgrims and the gypsies, after which the parade sets off again and returns to the church.

Address Place de l'Église, 13460 Les-Saintes-Maries-de-la-Mer | Directions Les-Saintes-Maries-de-la-Mer is in the Rhône delta, about 30 kilometres southeast of Arles, reached via the D 570. The church is in the town centre. | Tip Don't fail to climb up to the church roof: there is no better panoramic view anywhere in the Camargue.

61__ The Abbaye du Thoronet
Singing stones

Provence is blessed with many monasteries. Like a finely meshed network, stone witnesses to monastic life are spread across the region from Arles to Marseille and Saint-Maximin. Among all these abbeys, the three Cistercian monasteries in Provence – Sénanque, Silvacane and Thoronet – stand out for the clarity of their architecture.

"Being alone with oneself" – the practice of meditation in solitude, was praised by Saint Bernard of Clairvaux and is reflected in the remoteness of these abbeys; they are a manifestation of the return to poverty and simplicity, and with their functional character emphasise the role of physical labour in doing God's work. Even more than in the other abbeys, the monks of the Abbaye du Thoronet felt the obligation to live according to these self-imposed rules. Walls with decorations, sculptures and paintings were not favoured, as they could have distracted the monks from their prayers and choral singing.

Founded in 1136 in an insignificant side valley, the Abbaye du Thoronet is not only the oldest Cistercian monastery in Provence, it is also a particularly impressive expression of the Cistercian concept of plain "ascetic" architecture. Thanks to its short construction period, the monastery is a classic representation of the Romanesque style of building.

The perfection of the stonemasons' work is fascinating. The outer walls have joints without mortar, as in ancient times; this required great care because the surfaces had to be cut precisely – as can be seen on the façade of the monastery church. From one of the two church aisles, a door leads directly to the cloister and a broad stairway up to the dormitory, where the monks slept. It therefore took them only a few minutes to go down and celebrate Mass with the harmonies of their Gregorian chants.

Address On the D 79, 83340 Le Thoronet | **Directions** The Abbaye du Thoronet is five kilometres north-west of the village of Thoronet on the D 79, which in turn lies nine kilometres north-west of the motorway exit to Le Cannet (A 8). | **Opening times** April–Sept Mon–Sat 10am–6.30pm, Sun 10am–noon and 2–6.30pm, Oct–March Mon–Sat 10am–1pm and 2–5pm, Sun 10am–noon and 2–5pm | **Tip** The atmosphere is best early in the morning.

62__ The Mill Wheels
The Venice of Provence

There is splashing and bubbling everywhere in L'Isle-sur-la-Sorgue. Even the name is a reminder that the little town is surrounded like an island by the river Sorgue.

Originally L'Isle-sur-la-Sorgue was in the middle of a marshy area that was gradually drained by the building of many canals. Like an octopus, the Sorgue keeps the town in its grip, with watery tentacles that wind closely around the historic centre or pass right through it, and sometimes, as in the case with the Restaurant La Prévôté, impressively flow directly beneath buildings. The appearance of the town is characterised by numerous little bridges and restaurant terraces by the riverbank.

This enormous abundance of water was the basis of L'Isle-sur-la-Sorgue's prosperity. 150 years ago, 100 families of fishermen lived here and caught some 15,000 crabs in the Sorgue daily. An epidemic that devastated the crab population in 1884 was a severe blow to the town's main industry, and led to the ruin of the local fisheries.

Manufacturing was a further pillar of the economy. In the late Middle Ages there were more than a dozen paper and oil mills. They were later joined by several dyers' and weavers' workshops. At one time, there were approximately 70 large mill wheels powered by the waters of the Sorgue, and today six paddle-wheels with a thick covering of moss can still be admired along the boulevard that runs through the old quarter.

With so much water on all sides it seems logical that the annual celebrations of the French national holiday on 14 July should be marked in L'Isle-sur-la-Sorgue with a boat parade, boat jousting and a race around the old quarter on the water. On the following Sunday the fraternity of fishermen demonstrates how trout, eel and crabs used to be caught by fishermen standing on their flat-bottomed boats.

Address 84800 L'Isle-sur-la-Sorgue | Directions L'Isle-sur-la-Sorgue is 20 kilometres east of Avignon on the N 100. The mill wheels can be seen around the old quarter. | Tip The Sunday flea market in L'Isle-sur-la-Sorgue is the largest in Provence and definitely worth a visit.

63 The Cemetery
The Final Resting Place of Albert Camus

Lourmarin is nothing less than a holy place for lovers of literature. Albert Camus, the author of such famous novels as La Peste (The Plague) and L'Étranger (The Outsider) made it his home, and bought a house with the money he received for winning the Nobel Prize for Literature in 1957.

Camus never regretted his decision to move to Lourmarin, as the sun and the light reminded him of his childhood in Algiers, in the quarter Belcourt..

It was no coincidence that Camus chose Lourmarin: his teacher and friend Jean Grenier had written a book titled The Wisdom of Lourmarin, and invited him to stay there many times. When Camus came to visit in 1947, he noted in his diary: "Lourmarin. The first evening after so many years. The first star over the Luberon, the huge silence, the cypress whose tip quakes in the depths of my tiredness. A land, solemn and austere – despite its overwhelming beauty."

Unfortunately Camus was not able to enjoy his house for long, as he was killed in a road accident on 4 January 1960. He had let in the New Year in Lourmarin and was on his way back to Paris with Michel Gallimard, the nephew of his publisher, when a rear tire on the car burst and it smashed into a tree.

The house, still occupied by Camus' family, lies at an oblique angle to the road, which is now called Rue Albert Camus after its famous resident.

In order to keep away floods of visitors, the decision was made not to attach a memorial plaque to the house. A few worn steps lead up to a wooden front door from which the paint is peeling. Admirers of Camus, however, prefer to make a pilgrimage to the cemetery of Lourmarin. There one finds a plain gravestone, adorned with a lavender bush and bearing only the inscription: "Albert Camus 1913 – 1960."

Address Avenue Henri Bosco, 84160 Lourmarin | Directions Lourmarin is on the D 943 on the south slopes of the Luberon. The cemetery is at the south edge of the village. | Tip Another writer, Henri Bosco (1888–1976), is buried in the Lourmarin cemetery; Bosco is best known for his novel L'Ane Culotte.

64 Notre-Dame-de-Salagon
Healing plants and sarcophaguses

The land on which the former Benedictine abbey of Notre-Dame-de-Salagon is situated is one of the most historic sites in Haute-Provence. There was already a settlement here in Gallo-Roman times, and in late antiquity a funeral church was built – its foundations and sarcophaguses have been excavated. In the early 12th century Benedictine monks from Villeneuve-lès-Avignon founded a monastery here, which was soon one of the wealthiest in the region.

It seems unimaginable that the monastery was downgraded after the French Revolution to serve as a farmyard. Its buildings were used as barns and stalls for animals, and gradually decayed. Restoration work did not begin until 1955, and was recently completed with the construction of a visitor centre. Since 1981 the ethnological museum of the Département Haute-Provence has been housed here.

The most conspicuous sight is of course the monastery church, a plain late Romanesque building with harmonious proportions and an attractive doorway with round-headed arches. Inside the church, medieval frescoes have been preserved. In the monastery buildings, the everyday life of the abbey, from charcoal-burning to sheep-rearing to the cultivation of lavender, is presented in an interesting way, and several themed gardens surround the complex. Well over 600 kinds of herbs and healing plants are grown here, including such rare species as black bryony, southern wormwood (which was used as a laxative), and mandrake.

In one section of the garden, medieval plants and vegetables are cultivated, while the neighbouring "Jardin des Temps Modernes" with its brightly coloured and unusual borders is a source of inspiration for everyone who has a garden. A traditional farmhouse garden and a playfully conceived water garden with fruit trees round off the horticultural attractions.

Address 04300 Mane, www.musee-de-salagon.com | Directions Mane is three kilometres south of Forcalquier on the N 100, and the abbey lies one kilometre southwest of the village. The way there is signposted. | Opening times Daily June–Aug 10am–8pm; May, Sept 10am–7pm, Oct–April 10am–6pm | Tip A few hundred metres west of the monastery stands one of the loveliest Romanesque bridges in Provence.

65 Jean Giono's House

The desk of the Provençal Virgil

"I was born in Manosque and I have never left. The charm of the area is inexhaustible. When I say Manosque, strictly speaking I don't mean the town but the whole spectacle of hills and valleys in which the town lies and lives, the whole architecture of landscape from which it has derived its habits." With these words, the writer Jean Giono (1895–1970) erected a literary monument to his hometown.

To gain an impression of the beauty of Manosque, it is recommended to pay a visit to the home of Provence's most famous author.

High above the town, at the foot of Mont d'Or, Jean Giono bought a house with a large garden in 1929. It has remained unchanged since his death and is open to visitors. Its address alone, "Montée des Vraies Richesses," sounds like a little manifesto. A narrow path bordered by flowers, shrubs and an ivy-covered wall leads to a house adorned with green window shutters and roofed with round clay tiles.

The writer who was proclaimed by André Gide to be the "Virgil of Provence," lived in this house for more than four decades. Here he wrote his novels, including Jean le Bleu (Blue Boy), Le Grand Troupeau (To the Slaughterhouse) and Le Hussard sur le Toit (The Horseman on the Roof).

Visitors who climb the creaking stairs will find Giono's favourite study looking as if he had just stepped out for a moment. Even his gloves and an old skin coat are still lying on the settee. The spacious studio with its open fireplace and wine-red armchair for reading is bright and hospitable; bookshelves are crammed full and yellowing maps line the walls. On the desk lie the pipes of which he was so fond, and mementoes such as an Etruscan ring, ink pots and photographs. There is even a manuscript with hand-written corrections.

Address Montée des Vraies Richesses, 04100 Manosque | Directions Manosque has its own exit on highway A 51 (follow the signs). The house is in the Lou Paraïs district. The footpath branches off from Montée des Vraies Richesses. | Opening times Fri 2.30–5pm, Tue–Thu 2–5pm by previous arrangement: tel. 0033/0492877303 | Tip There is a permanent exhibition about Giono in the Centre Jean Giono on Boulevard Elémir Bourges; www.centrejeangiono.com.

66__ Cabanons
Fishermen's huts with atmosphere

Marseille is a sprawling monster and a great vibrant port with all the temptations that characterise a large Mediterranean city. Fortunately a few hidden gems have been preserved – for example the cabanons, tiny weekend houses that are at least as typical of Marseille as its famous bouillabaisse.

Originally a cabanon was a summerhouse where the people of the city would meet on Sundays and during the holidays in order to enjoy their natural surroundings, allowing the course of the day to be determined only by the rhythm of the sun. In the evenings they all gathered around a long table and enjoyed a delicious meal, usually prepared with freshly caught fish.

The first cabanons were built at the end of the 19th century, when the city was becoming ever larger and more prosperous. They were not, however, an indulgence of the rich, but an important expression of the leisure habits of all social classes. The houses did not provide decadent accommodations but were basic wooden huts with a veranda, and possessed neither running water nor an electricity supply. With their plain form, the cabanons resembled boat sheds, and were filled with tables, chairs, cushions, crockery, gas stoves, mattresses and sunshades – in other words, with everything that you need to spend a day beside the sea.

Along the coast of the Mediterranean Sea, which extends to the east of the city from the Vallon des Auffes as far as the calanques, there were once more than 1000 of these huts, many of them built in an uncontrolled way, covering hillsides around the rocky bays. As a consequence of the construction boom during the post-war years, Marseille swallowed up much of the surrounding area. The result is that most of the cabanons have disappeared today. Nevertheless, many of those that remain can still be found in Les Goudes and Callelongue.

Address Les Goudes, 13008 Marseille | Directions Bus no. 19 from Station Castellane to Madrague; from there bus no. 20 to Les Goudes and Callelongue. | Tip It is worth going to La Grotte, a beautiful restaurant with a Baroque dining room in the Calanque de Callelongue; www.lagrotte-13.com.

67 _ Cité Radieuse

Le Corbusier's machine for living

Cité Radieuse is anchored on Boulevard Michelet like a beached ocean liner. Designed by the Swiss architect Le Corbusier (1887 – 1965), the dimensions alone of this unité d'habitation (housing unit) on stilts are enormous: Cité Radieuse is 165 metres long, 24 metres wide and 56 metres high!

But Corbusier would not have been Corbusier if the design had not been pursuing a special architectural vision: his aim was not only to build an autonomous vertical city that included a street of shops, a crèche for children, and a gymnasium on the roof, but also to do this while maximizing as small an area as possible.

Altogether he planned 337 apartments of varying sizes for 1500 people, all of them extending over two storeys and each having an extremely large window, measuring 3.66 metres by 4.80 metres, and their own terrace.

The people of Marseille found little to like about the building, and after its completion in 1952 even called it the "Maison de Fada" (the Madman's House).

Originally Cité Radieuse was primarily intended as social housing for poor families, but soon it became trendy to live in a house built by Le Corbusier. Many of the maisonettes were turned into owner-occupied properties, and the residents now include numerous well-to-do families and artists, who appreciate the light-flooded rooms.

Anyone who is interested in Cité Radieuse can visit the interior of the complex without difficulty: simply walk inside and take the lift to the third floor, which was conceived as a shopping arcade – in addition to a hotel, it also accommodates a bakery and a food market – or go all the way up to the roof terrace. The attraction here at the top of the building is a fantastic viewing platform that includes a pool of water.

Address 280, Boulevard Michelet, 13008 Marseille, www.marseille-citeradieuse.org |
Directions Métro 2 too Métro-Station Rond-Point-du-Prado, then bus no. 21 to Cité
Radieuse. | Tip Le Corbusier, the two-star hotel in Cité Radieuse, has retained its
authentic atmosphere; www.hotellecorbusier.com.

68_ The Island
The hole leading to freedom

There is a long tradition of locking up prisoners on islands, where they can be watched over without a great effort, and escape is very difficult. Along with Robben Island and Alcatraz, the Île d'If is among the oldest and most infamous prison islands, and the Château d'If was long seen as a symbol of arbitrary state power.

In the early 16th century King François I ordered the barren rocky island to be made into a fortress – not to serve as a prison, but to give Marseille better protection from attack by ships. Already in 1634 the Île d'If was converted into a state prison, as the absolutist rulers of France had many enemies.

Originally these were mainly Protestants and revolutionary zealots who rebelled against the church, king or state. Later it was de-serters and – after the French Revolution – royalists who languished in the gloom of the dungeons. The punishment was often out of all proportion to the crime: one Glandevès de Niozelles once served six years in penance for the transgression of failing to doff his hat to Louis XIV.

Until 1872 the limestone island was used almost without inter-ruption as a jail. Thousands upon thousands of inmates suffered a miserable existence, locked up in inhumane conditions. Ironically, the best-known prisoner never set foot on the island. This was Ed-mond Dantès, the "Count of Monte Christo." In 1845 Alexandre Dumas the Elder made the Château d'If the setting of one of the most widely read novels in the world.

Following the abandonment of the state prison, the island, made famous by The Count of Monte Christo, was turned into a strange sightseeing destination. To this day the innumerable names of pris-oners, scratched into the walls of the cells, sends a shiver down the visitor's spine. And of course the famous hole between the two cells can also be seen …

Address Île d'If, 13001 Marseille | Directions Every day many boats make the trip from the Vieux Port to the Château d'If (15 minutes' crossing time). | Opening times April–Sept Tue–Sun 9.30am–6.30pm, Oct–March 9.30am–5.30pm | Tip A boat ticket also takes you to the Îles du Frioul, a good place for swimming.

69 Monument aux morts de l'Armée d'Orient

For the fallen of the Army of the Orient

Marseille is regarded as the gateway to the Orient. In Roman times and during the Middle Ages, there was a lively trade and exchange with lands on the other side of the Mediterranean. Later, in the colonial era, the eyes of France were directed, as a matter of course, towards Algeria, Tunisia and Morocco. In Senegal and Gabon, too, raw materials and political influence were coveted.

During the First World War, France inevitably came into conflict with Germany in Africa – it was, as the name indicates, a global war, and fierce battles were not only fought in Flanders and Champagne, but also in Africa, where France was primarily interested in extending its colonial possessions.

The result of these clashes was that the German Empire lost all of its African colonies, while France honoured those members of its Army of the Orient who fell in this cause by erecting a huge monument. It was unveiled in 1927 in a solemn ceremony next to the waterfront road in Marseille.

Even from a distance this gigantic arch is clearly visible. At its centre stands a bronze female figure with her arms raised high – a symbol of victory and triumph. The arch is flanked by stone-carved soldiers, while the names and dates of the major campaigns are inscribed on the sides of the monument. The arch purposely guides the viewer's gaze towards the Orient, and steps lead directly down to the sea behind the monument.

In keeping with the French's pride in fallen military heroes, this place of commemoration was elevated by the state to the rank of a monument historique in 2011. This confers on it the same status as the palace of the popes in Avignon and the basilica of Notre-Dame de la Garde.

AUX HEROS DE L'ARMEE D'ORIENT ET DES TERRES LOINTAINES

Address Corniche du Président John F. Kennedy, 13007 Marseille | Directions Bus no. 83 to Vallon des Auffes. | Tip Directly behind the monument lie the Îles du Frioul, which can be reached in half an hour by boat from the Vieux Port.

70__The Quartier du Panier

The beating heart of Marseille is behind the harbour

Harbour districts have an unsavoury reputation all over the world, and Marseille's has long been especially notorious. Its narrow alleyways were always known for poverty, crime and prostitution. Many writers in the early 20th century, from Vladimir Nabokov to Ernst Jünger, were fascinated and repelled in equal measure by the stench and noise of this quarter: stray dogs and half-naked children played between piles of refuse, while behind frayed curtains whole ship's crews took their pleasure with ladies of easy virtue.

Then came the Second World War. After the Germans marched into the south of France, which had remained unoccupied until then, SS Reichsführer Heinrich Himmler ordered the "clearing out of this nest of French criminals" by means of "radical blowing up." In the space of 17 days in February 1943, following the evacuation of its inhabitants, the whole harbour quarter of almost 1500 houses was reduced to rubble.

Fortunately, parts of the Quartier du Panier, which lay on higher ground behind the port, were spared this barbaric destruction. This district, simply referred to as "Panier" by the locals, is delightful for its original atmosphere and maritime character. The hills of the Quartier du Panier are the place where the city of Marseille originated.

The rectangular Place de Lenche probably marks the site of the Greek marketplace, the agora. To the south of it, remains of the ancient Greek theatre were excavated.

In the alleys, which are largely free of motorised traffic, many little junk shops and food stores can be found, as well as cafés and bars frequented by the locals; there are hidden passageways such as the Passage de Lorette, while here and there the street scene opens up onto little squares like the Place des Moulins, which was once known for its windmills.

Address 13002 Marseille | Directions The Quartier du Panier is on a slight elevation, about five minutes' walk north of the harbour, near the Metro stop National (M2). | Tip La Navette Marseillaise: this bakery at no. 68 Rue Caisserie sells biscuits made in the traditional manner with dough containing olive oil and white wine in addition to butter and eggs; www.les-navettes-des-accoules.fr.

71__ Savon de Marseille

Soap from olive oil

As long ago as the late Middle Ages, the soap makers of Marseille were held in high regard. Louis XIV was especially interested in soap from Marseille. He brought in soap-makers from Genoa and ordered that their products should not contain any animal fat. Since those days, therefore, nothing but pure olive oil has been used to manufacture the soap. The industry soon developed into a pillar of the economy. Savon de Marseille was exported as far as North Africa and the Middle East.

The 19th century is regarded as the golden age of soap-making in Marseille. For a time more than 100 soap factories were in operation in Provence. Later, cheap industrial mass production caused the decline of the industry, and by the turn of the new millennium no more than five traditional soap makers remained in the city.

Fortunately the famous Savon de Marseille has enjoyed a comeback in recent years.

Purchasers appreciate the product for its high proportion of olive oil (at least 72 percent) and the pleasant scent of the healing herbs and spices that are added to the soap; no dyes or surface active agents are used. Savon de Marseille is also fully biodegradable, and therefore a green product.

In the elaborate manufacturing process, olive oil is boiled with caustic soda until – with the addition of sea salt – crude soap has been created. This is then washed repeatedly in order to remove the soda. Next the soap substance is separated, dried in the mistral wind and cut into cubes or rectangular pieces. After a further drying process that lasts two weeks, the six sides of the block of soap are imprinted with the traditional stamp "Savon de Marseille" and the maker's name.

The Savonnerie Marseillaise de la Licorne sells its famous products directly on the south shore of the Vieux Port.

24, Quai Rive Neuve, 13007 Marseille | Directions Savonnerie de la Licorne
is next to the Metro station Vieux Port (M 1). | Tip Production on Cours Julien can
be watched from Monday to Saturday at 11am, 3pm and 4pm;
www.savon-de-marseille-licorne.com.

72__Vallon des Auffes
A mini-harbour in a city of millions

For two millennia Marseille has been the most important French port on the Mediterranean coast. The Vieux Port was not only the cradle of the city – to this day it is the tourist heart of Marseille. The small harbour in Vallon des Auffes, by contrast, lying a little bit off the beaten track, is mostly known only to locals, and travellers seldom find their way here.

Vallon des Auffes has remained a traditional fishing port to the present day. With its boats, small fishermen's houses, and restaurants, it seems like an oasis of calm amidst the bustling activity of Marseille, a city of more than one million inhabitants.

Originally Vallon des Auffes was a rocky bay, like the famous calanques of Cassis, but in the 19th century, when the coast road was built, its shores were covered in concrete. Luckily the mood of this picture-book harbour was preserved, as the Corniche road bypasses Vallon via a bridge. Hidden steps lead down to a harbour full of atmosphere, and the site has been used more than once as a film set, for example for the action movie "French Connection," made in 1971.

For gastronomic reasons, too, it is worth visiting Vallon des Auffes, as no less than three outstanding restaurants have set up here: Pizzeria Chez Jeannot with its family character, Chez Fonfon, and the Michelin-starred L'Epusiette. The second and third of these are excellent places to sample the famous Provençal bouillabaisse, as here you can be absolutely certain that the fish has been freshly caught.

The ingredients considered to be essential in bouillabaisse are red racasse, gurnard (grondin), European conger eels (congre) and other, smaller fish similar to perch; neither langoustines nor shellfish should find their way into an "authentic" bouillabaisse, by the way.

Address Vallon des Auffes, 13007 Marseille | **Directions** Vallon des Auffes is about three kilometres east of Marseille harbour, easily reached on bus no. 83. | **Tip** The half-hour walk right on the waterfront promenade to the Vieux Port is wonderful, with fantastic views of the sea and Château d'If.

73 Massif de la Sainte-Baume

The grotto of Mary Magdalene

For centuries the people of Provence and Burgundy have been disputing the question of where the mortal remains of Mary Magdalene were laid to rest. Whereas Vézelay on the Way of St James insists that the relics of this saint were taken to Burgundy as long ago as the 9th century in order to protect them from the Saracens, the people of Provence point to the basilica of Saint-Maximin-La-Sainte-Baume. It is said that Mary Magdalene is buried in the crypt there, along with her servant woman Marzelle, and their two companions, Maximin and Sidonius. In 1279 Charles II of Anjou is reported to have personally discovered four sarcophaguses during excavations here. One of them contained the bones of the saints, it was ascertained at that time – presumably with the aid of genetic analysis, or a similarly reliable method, or a "feeling" …

Insofar as one is prepared to believe the Christian legends, it is fortunately not in dispute that Mary Magdalene spent the last 30 years of her life in a grotto on the north flank of the Massif de la Sainte-Baume. Mentioned in all gospels as a witness of the resurrection of Jesus Christ and as one of his followers, she withdrew to the solitude of the massif in order to do penance in this barren place, as she is said to have worked as a prostitute previously.

The name of the striking mountain ridge, which runs east to west only a few kilometres from the coast, is derived from "Baoumo," the Provençal word for grotto. The short but steep ascent to the grotto is strenuous but rewarding! Since the Middle Ages, the cave has been a popular place of pilgrimage – Mary Magdalene is revered as the patron saint of women, of the seduced, and of penitent sinners.

From here a good hour's walk on a long-distance path marked in red and white takes you to the 1148-metre-high Joug de l'Aigle.

Address Massif de la Sainte-Baume | Directions The massif lies 30 kilometres east of Aubagne. There is a walkers' car park on the D 92, 400 metres east of the Hôtellerie de la Sainte-Baume. | Opening times Daily 8am–6pm, Mass at 11am | Tip The basilica of Saint-Maximin-La-Sainte-Baume (20 kilometres northeast) is the largest Gothic church in Provence. Its nave is almost 30 metres high!

74 Marais du Vigueirat

An ornithological paradise in Provence

The Camargue has an ecosystem unique in Europe, but is not easily accessible to visitors due to strict regulations that protect the nature reserve. Rare species of birds such as grey herons and kingfishers can hatch their eggs here undisturbed, as no one except authorised botanists and zoologists are permitted to enter its core zone; everyone else is only allowed to visit its margins.

This makes it all the more appealing to explore the Marais du Vigueirat on the eastern edge of the Camargue. This marsh area covering more than 1000 hectares lies a little south of the hamlet of Mas-Thibert.

In the 1980s it was acquired by the Conservatoire du Littoral in order to enable anyone who's interested to get to know the flora and fauna of the Camargue and the adjoining Crau.

The nature reserve is home to about 280 bird species, of which 80 also nest there – such as all nine types of heron found in Europe, including the rare purple heron. Visitors with some knowledge of ornithology can spot the bittern, stilt, moustached warbler, lapwing, European bee-eater, common shelduck, avocet and black kite through their binoculars.

The Marais du Vigueirat can be explored from a carriage, as part of a guided tour or individually. Four hides and two towers enable visitors to observe the animals and plants while disturbing the biotope as little as possible. An extremely enjoyable 3.5-kilometre circular route (sentier des cabanes) leads through the marshland, partly on raised boardwalks. It is an accessible path, and therefore suitable for wheelchairs and children's strollers.

As a further attraction, it is possible to taste a kind of crayfish caught by the local fishermen: the red swamp crawfish, an invasive species that was introduced from North America and has multiplied in this habitat.

Address Mas-Thibert, 13104 Arles, www.marais-vigueirat.reserves-naturelles.org | Directions Mas-Thibert is 20 kilometres southeast of Arles on the left bank of the Rhône, reached via the D 35. The nature reserve is signposted. | Opening times Feb–Nov daily 10am–5pm; April–Sept daily guided tours at 10.30am and 2.30pm, carriage rides at 10am and 3pm | Tip In summer bring protection against mosquitoes.

75_ The Glacières
Natural freezers

Natural freezers in Provence? The sceptical may furrow their brows or shake their heads, but in fact there really are several dozen so-called glacières in the hills of Provence. In the past, as in our day, people longed for cooling ice and cold drinks during the hot summer months.

The greatest concentration of icehouses in the whole Mediterranean region can be found in the Massif de la Saint-Baume. Between the 16th and 19th centuries more than a dozen of them were constructed in order to supply ice to the aristocracy and the wealthy middle classes.

For this purpose icehouses were hewn out of the rock, usually reaching a depth of up to 15 metres, while others were built with stone walls. In order to stop the ice from melting quickly, the icehouses were covered with a vaulted roof insulated with sand. The ice was produced by diverting spring water along channels into shallow artificial pools up in the mountains. As soon as the water had frozen, blocks of ice were cut out of the pools and then dragged on wooden boards along paths known as "Chemins de la Glace" to the icehouses, where they could be stored for several months.

According to demand they were then transported by night in specially made, closed carriages to customers in Marseille, Toulon or Aix-en-Provence to be used in the preparation of desserts or cooling drinks.

Access is difficult to most of the glacières. An exception to this is the Glacière de Pivaut, which is situated only about 100 metres from a road and was restored at some expense a few years ago. With its height of 23 metres and diameter of 19 metres it is also the largest icehouse in the whole Massif de la Sainte-Baume! Its capacity is an impressive 3600 cubic metres. Information panels provide an excellent explanation of how this "freezer" worked.

Address 83136 Mazaugues | Directions The Glacière de Pivaut lies seven kilometres west of Mazaugues on the road to Plan d'Aups. There is a large car park on the road and the short path to the glacière is signposted. | Opening times Accessible all year | Tip The Musée de la Glace in Mazaugues provides information about ice-making; http://museedelaglace.free.fr.

76 Les Pénitents des Mées

Penance in stone

Let's be honest: when summer has undeniably arrived in Provence, when the temperature slowly but surely approaches 30 degrees Celsius and skirts get shorter from day to day, what man can resist taking a peek – sometimes secretively, sometimes more openly – at a few shapely female legs?

At the start of the 6th century this is supposedly what happened with a group of monks. Sweating under their habits, they were on the road for a pilgrimage or some other mission (the legend is silent about the exact reason for their trip) when, not far from Les Mées, they encountered a good number of lightly clad women. No one who is familiar with the women of Provence will fail to understand that in such a case it is necessary to stop for a short rest.

There was just one person who was displeased by this brief appreciation of the glory of God's creation: the hermit Saint Donatus is reported to have been red-faced with anger, and in punishment for gazing back at the women with lustful eyes, he turned the monks to stone.

Whatever you might think of the legend, the sheer, monumental columns of rock that rise in the valley of the Durance are without a doubt an extremely striking feature of the landscape. The bizarrely shaped rock massif with a width of one kilometre that lies directly behind the village of Mées was formed over the last 25 million years through erosion and sedimentation. The cyclopean penitents' columns consist of a particularly resistant kind of rock and thus defied the effects of erosion.

At their highest point the Pénitents des Mées reach 114 metres above the valley floor. The rock formation can be explored on a walking trail marked with a horizontal yellow line. This almost eight-kilometre-long "Circuit des Pénitents" is clearly signposted throughout, and passes a campsite on its way up to the plateau.

Address 04190 Les Mées | Directions Les Mées is 20 kilometres south of Sisteron in the Durance valley, easily reached via the A 51 and N 85. | Tip The main sight in Les Mées is the 16th-century Église Notre-Dame de l'Olivier, whose tower is topped by a typically Provençal bell cage.

77 Lonely Mountain Range

Alone with snake eagles and ravens

The Montagne de Lure is one of Provence's little-known mountain ranges, and has thus remained largely undeveloped for tourism. When car-parking spaces at the summit of Mont Ventoux become scarce in summer, it is still pleasantly lonely on the ridges of the Montagne de Lure.

There is no question that Mont Ventoux is almost 100 metres higher, but the 1826 metres of the Montagne de Lure also amount to a respectable altitude. The higher you climb in the Lure range, the more rugged and barren the landscape. Juniper heath and fields of scree with sparse vegetation dominate the scenery. High up on the summit of the range, which runs from west to east, stand the transmitter masts of the Signal de Lure. The breathtaking panorama extends from Mont Ventoux to the Maritime Alps and the Pic de Bure to the northeast.

An inhospitable wind often blows here, which makes the diversity of vegetation and bird life surprising. Walkers who keep their eyes open on the ridges at heights of 1300 to 1800 metres can spot gentians, primulas, blue thistles and mountain tulips, as well as the pale yellow elder-flowered orchid and other species of orchid. Snake eagles circle majestically in the sky, and the north slopes are nesting grounds for the rare northern raven, the largest species of raven found in Europe.

On the south slopes of the Montagne de Lure there are six upland pastures, for example the Jas de Pierrefeu and the Jas de Marguerier. This type of pasture is uncharacteristic of Provence, and the land is not in use any longer. At a height of more than 1200 metres the church of Notre-Dame-de-Lure, a monastery of the Order of Chalais founded in 1165, is hidden away beneath ancient lime and walnut trees. The plain and austere-looking church is a reminder of the hardships endured by the monks who sought a retreat in the solitude of Haute-Provence and in their strong faith.

Address Montagne de Lure | **Directions** The Montagne de Lure lies 20 kilometres south-west of Sisteron. Only one road (D 53 or D 113) crosses the range, almost reaching the summit. | **Tip** On 15 August (the Ascension of the Virgin) the former monastery is the destination for a pilgrimage, and Mass is celebrated in the church.

78 Cézannes Mountain

To be born here is to be lost

"I've bought the Montagne Sainte-Victoire." With these words Pablo Picasso is said to have surprised his friend, the art dealer Daniel-Henry Kahnweiler, in 1958. Thinking that Picasso had bought a painting by Cézanne, Kahnweiler responded: "Congratulations – but which one?" Picasso had to clear up the misunderstanding and convince Kahnweiler that he had not bought a picture but the Château de Vauvenargues, along with 800 hectares of land. His plan was to live and work there on the northern margins of the Montagne Sainte-Victoire.

The Montagne Sainte-Victoire is not only a conspicuous limestone massif rising to a height of just over 1000 metres, east of Aix-en-Provence, but probably also the most significant mountain in art history. Paul Cézanne painted more than 80 watercolours and oil paintings of this mountain, constantly striving to find "constructions and harmonies parallel to nature." Cézanne, who hailed from Aix, had an aversion to provincial attitudes. He deplored the narrow-mindedness of his fellow men, yet he loved the villages of Provence, the coast around Marseille, and, above all, the Montagne Sainte-Victoire: "To be born here is to be lost. Nothing else ever pleases one."

In November 1901 Cézanne bought a piece of land on a hill north of the city in order to build a house with a studio according to his own designs. He had chosen the site on Chemin de Lauves well – from here he could quickly walk to his beloved Montagne Sainte-Victoire. Almost every morning Cézanne set off to capture on canvas this mountain, which has the appearance of a gigantic wave, frozen in position shortly before it breaks. In autumn 1906 Cézanne was caught by a storm while out painting and was found in a state of hypothermia; he caught pneumonia and died a few days later.

Address Montagne Sainte-Victoire | **Directions** The Montagne Sainte-Victoire and Vauvenargues are to the east of Aix-en-Provence on the D 10. From the hamlet of Les Cabassols a long-distance trail marked in white and red leads to the summit, a climb of two hours. | **Tip** Cézanne's studio, preserved in its original condition, can be visited in Avenue Paul Cézanne in Aix-en-Provence; www.atelier-cezanne.com.

79__The Cyclists' Mountain

55 minutes to the summit

Mont Ventoux is exactly 1912 metres high. Its bare summit, visible from far away, dominates a large area of Provence. This mountain offers a truly magical attraction for bike riders, so it may come as a surprise to learn that the first man known to have reached the top was not Eddy Merckx, but the poet Petrarch in 1336. Today Mont Ventoux is ascended by many more cyclists than walkers – every day hundreds of bikers with sporting ambitions set out on the arduous, perspiration-inducing route.

In 1951 Mont Ventoux was included in the itinerary of the Tour de France for the first time, and has now long been established as an outstanding section of the race. The peloton has climbed the mountain 14 times altogether. The record is held by the Basque cyclist Iban Mayo, who covered the distance from Bédoin to the summit in only 55 minutes and 51 seconds in 2004. Those with a good state of fitness can be proud if they manage the 22-kilometre stretch with its climb of 1610 metres in less than two hours. In contrast to Iban Mayo, Lance Armstrong, and many other record-holders whose fabulous times were achieved thanks to various chemical and pharmaceutical substances, the brave amateurs who flock to Mont Ventoux and labour up the hairpin bends without the assistance of performance-enhancing drugs are truly to be applauded. They have to overcome gradients of up to nine percent – without the protection of any shade.

Two kilometres from the top a short break is an obligatory part of the programme: a memorial stone decorated with wheel-rims, spokes and other bike equipment commemorates the British cyclist Tom Simpson, who collapsed and died on 13 July 1967 while attempting – with the help of amphetamines and alcohol – to conquer Mont Ventoux on one of the hottest days of the tour. His last words are said to have been: "Put me back on the bloody bike."

Address Mont Ventoux | **Directions** The D 974 first of all leads east from Bédoin, then right over the summit in an east-west direction. | **Tip** Those who come without their own bike can rent one in Bédoin at the foot of Mont Ventoux: La Route du Ventoux, tel. 0033/0490670740, ww.francebikerentals.com.

80   The Golden Star

Who hung the chain across the gorge?

Moustiers-Sainte-Marie in Haute-Provence is mainly known for its faiences, which have been produced here for centuries. In the age of the Sun King Louis XIV, Provençal faiences were among the most sought-after in the kingdom of France.

It is well worth making a trip to Moustiers, which is among "Les Plus Beaux Villages de France." With an imposing rocky backdrop, the village church and a few dozen old stone houses huddle together in the shape of an amphitheatre, while a wild mountain stream rushes through the middle.

Those who fail to raise their eyes heavenwards in the narrow alleyways can easily overlook the greatest mystery in this village: the gorge of Moustiers is spanned by a 227-metre-long cast-iron chain, from the middle of which dangles a golden five-pointed star. Strangely, no documents or other sources report who stretched this chain weighing 150 kilograms across the gap, or when and why it was done.

According to a legend recounted by Frédéric Mistral, this so-called "Chaîne de l'Etoile" was donated by a knight of the Order of St John named Blacas who came from Moustiers-Sainte-Marie. Blacas – it is reported – fell into the hands of the Saracens in around the year 1210 while on crusade and swore that if he were ever freed from captivity, he would suspend a star in honour of the holy Virgin Mary above the gorge in his hometown.

Doubts about the truth of this story cannot be suppressed, however, if one takes a close look at a painting by an anonymous master in the Poor Souls' Chapel of the Romanesque parish church of Notre-Dame-de-l'Assomption. The picture, painted in 1482, is an extremely accurate landscape view of Moustiers – but the eye-catching chain and the star do not appear in it! The question therefore remains unresolved: who hung the chain across the gorge?

Address 04360 Moustiers-Sainte-Marie | Directions Moustiers-Sainte-Marie is on the D 952 to the west of the Grand Canyon du Verdon. | Tip The Musée Historique de la Faïence in historic vaults beneath the vicarage presents a selection of regional faïences, daily except Tuesday.

81__The Ruined Village
Gazing into the abyss

The Luberon is known for pretty villages that have largely been able to preserve their authentic charm. Wealthy Parisians and artists, for example the former French minister of culture, Jack Lang, and the actor John Malkovich, have been enthusiastic about this part of Provence for many years. The result is that property prices have risen dramatically in recent years, and houses in villages like Lourmarin and Ménerbes have become unaffordable for most.

Oppède-le-Vieux is the only place free from the real-estate boom, as this village on the north slopes of the Luberon consists mostly of ruins.

The majority of its inhabitants left in the late 19th century in order to build a new Oppède down in the valley. In 1936 only ten people still lived in the dilapidated village, where the houses are stacked up the slope towards a crumbling castle built by the counts of Toulouse in the 13th century. Only the Romanesque church of Notre-Dame d'Alidon remained generally intact.

A small number of houses in the lower part of the village have been renovated and made habitable again – and a village bistro has even opened up – but in the maze of alleys that is the upper part of the village, many gaps without their windows and empty arches are picturesquely open to the Provençal sky. Handsome Renaissance façades can be seen again and again, while the former town hall still has its attractive campanile.

It is not difficult to clamber around the overgrown walls of the old castle, though a degree of caution should be exercised, as the rock falls away vertically in several places. Unless you have a good head for heights it is wise to stay away from the most spectacular view on offer in Oppède-le-Vieux: through a hole in the exposed latrine of the château you can look down more than 30 metres into an abyss.

Address Oppède-le-Vieux, 84580 Oppède | Directions Oppède-le-Vieux is some eleven kilometres east of Cavaillon and is reached via the D 2 and D 176. | Tip Directly beneath the village lies an attractive landscape garden. A wide range of Provençal flora, including herbs, flourishes on its 15 terraces.

82__The Statue of Augustus

Marble thanks to the founder of the city

Augustus looks small, almost delicate, when you look at him from the upper tiers of the ancient theatre in Orange. Standing in the middle of the back wall of the stage, he raises his right arm in greeting. It is only when you examine the dimensions that you realise that the emperor is more than three and a half metres tall.

The fragments of this marble statue were found by chance in 1931 during excavation work, and had to be painstakingly reconstructed before they could be returned to their prominent position between the stumps of two columns.

The statue depicts Augustus as a victorious general in his parade uniform, while at the same time glorifying him as a peace-bringing ruler, as he is shown with a bare head and without weapons. The unknown sculptor took his cue from the classical forms of Greek statues by presenting Augustus as the ideal of the serious-minded and god-fearing man.

The earliest inhabitants of Orange had a close relationship to the Roman emperor, as they were veterans of the 2nd Legion. Taking its name from a Celtic god of a water spring, Orange became one of the richest and most magnificent cities in the province of Gallia Narbonensis.

Along with the triumphal arch, the theatre has been a UNESCO World Heritage site since 1981, and is an impressive demonstration of the significance theatre had in the everyday life of the Romans. The building was used as the public venue for the mixture of religious ceremonies and entertainment that was so highly regarded in Roman times.

The theatre in Orange, which held up to 10,000 spectators, was skilfully constructed on the slope of a hill so that the stage wall is as high as the topmost tier of the auditorium, and the building thus appears to be entirely closed from the outside.

Address 84100 Orange, www.theatre-antique.com | Directions Orange is easy to reach via the A 7. The ancient theatre is in the middle of the town. | Opening times June–Aug daily 9am–7pm, April, May, Sept daily 9am–6pm, March, Oct 9am–5.30pm, Nov–Feb 9.30am–4.30pm | Tip The Musée d'Art et d'Histoire diagonally opposite the theatre displays archaeological finds and precious floor mosaics.

83 The Jardin de Val Joanis
Wine-making and horticulture

Although Provence is a sun-kissed region that never fails to charm travellers, strangely it possesses few large gardens. One exception is the Jardin de Val Joanis on the southern edge of the Luberon.

In 1978 its former owner, Cécile Chancel, decided to lay out a garden at her country estate and called in the eminent landscape designer Tobbie Loup de Viane.

The result is a French garden in the 18th-century style with the addition, in accordance with Provençal tradition, of a small olive grove and a rectangular pond.

The design gained official recognition when French garden journalists voted the Jardin de Val Joanis "garden of the year" in 2008.

In a valley sheltered from the mistral wind, the garden extends over three terraces. One is a vegetable garden interspersed with healing herbs, where ornamental cabbage grows next to artichokes. The other two terraces are reserved for extensive flower beds and fruit trees. Lilies and euphorbia add spots of colour – a true paradise for the senses!

There is also a shady bower on which roses and other flowering climbing plants entwine, and yew trees clipped in the shape of slender cones that lend a structure to the garden layout.

Yet Val Joanis is more than just a wonderful garden. It is also one of the largest and best-known vineyards in the Luberon. On an area amounting to more than 400 hectares, the grapes for high-quality white, rosé and red wines are cultivated.

The emphasis is on grape varieties that are native to this soil – for example Syrah, Grenache and Mourvèdre. Even the highly critical wine guru Robert Parker compared the Réserve les Griottes, which is matured for several months in oak barrels, to an outstanding Châteauneuf-du-Pape!

Address 84120 Pertuis, www.val-joanis.com | Directions The Jardin de Val Joanis lies three kilometres west of Pertuis and is clearly signposted from the D973 leading to Cavaillon. | Opening times July, Aug 10am–7pm, April–Oct 10am–1pm and 2–7pm | Tip In July and August there is a guided tour of the wine cellars on Thursdays at 4pm.

84_ The Crocodile Farm

Reptiles in water from cooling towers

A lot of water is needed in the operation of a nuclear power plant in order to moderate the heat constantly released by fission in the reactor, which is why plants and their massive cooling towers are always built right next to a river. This is the case with Tricastin, which uses water from the Rhône.

For a few years the water that was warmed in this way was simply channelled back into the Rhône, until an ingenious businessman hit on the idea of using it in a crocodile farm. Now more than 400 crocodiles live on an area of 6500 square metres in the enormous hothouse of the Ferme aux Crocodiles, which opened in 1990. They include rare species, such as the Indian gharial with its long, thin jaws. The air in the hothouse is tropical and humid. There are several lakes, an artificial waterfall and a section with giant tortoises and tropical birds, as well as an "African" village with houses built on stilts.

In 2010 an open-air compound of 4000 square metres was added to the farm so that the crocodiles and tortoises could lounge in the sun in the summer months.

The farm is unique in Europe. The animals are not kept behind glass but are separated by means of ditches and high parapets from visitors, who therefore have the impression of being in the middle of the action.

Sluggish, sometimes with their mouths wide open, the enormous reptiles lie on the beach or drift in the water, almost motionless. Some of them are as much as seven metres long. Only at feeding time does it become clear how agile they can be.

Information panels in several languages explain how the crocodiles are bred and how they live – for example the fact that the animals usually live in a harem, with one male having an average of nine females.

Address Les Blachettes, 26700 Pierrelatte, www.lafermeauxcrocodiles.com | **Directions** The crocodile farm is south of Pierrelatte, about ten minutes from the A 7, exit to Bollène or Montélimar Sud. | **Opening times** Daily March–Sept 9.30am–7pm, Oct–Feb 9.30am–5pm; feeding times: crocodiles 3pm, tortoises 11am | **Tip** 20 kilometres south of Pierrelatte at Pont St. Esprit is one of the oldest bridges across the Rhône.

85__The Infinite Beach

A Paradise, not only for nudists

Provence has a coastline of more than 200 kilometres, with countless wonderful sandy beaches. Whereas on the eastern section of the coast most of the beaches are small and framed by bays, in the Camargue, those seeking long walks in the sand will find exactly what they are looking for. The Plage de Piémançon, located about an hour's drive from Arles at the end of a dead-end road, has a certain cult status.

Past the saltworks of Salin-de-Giraud a little road winds between the salt lakes. To the left and right a few flamingos wade in the shallow water. Apart from a causeway here and there, the land is as flat as a board. Seemingly at the end of the world, the road finally brings you to the Plage de Piémançon, a superb beach that is also popularly known as the Plage d'Arles.

There are no facilities here whatsoever, but plenty of wind and a sandy beach that stretches out endlessly and is several hundred metres wide in places. It gives you a real Robinson Crusoe feeling. Many owners of campervans and caravans choose this place for a holiday, and camp at the end of the access road – although there is neither drinking water here nor a power supply or amenities of any other kind. Various types of seagulls and terns nest in the dunes, while the beach is the domain of windsurfers and kite surfers, who find ideal conditions here for their sport. If you walk a little way eastwards, a sign bears the inscription "Ici on vit nu" ("Here we live nude"), indicating that you need have no inhibitions about taking off your clothes.

Further west, reached by a gravelled access road from Salin-de-Giraud, lies the Plage de Beauduc, site of an illegal but tolerated caravan village, where some people live all year round. Its residents try to shelter themselves from the wind by erecting strange structures made from driftwood and straw matting.

Address Plage de Piémançon | **Directions** The Plage de Piémançon is 15 kilometres south of Salin-de-Giraud at the end of the D36. | **Tip** There is no shade, and the wind is often too strong for a parasol, so bring sunblock with a high protection factor.

86 __Musée de Préhistoire

A walk through the prehistoric world

Early humans seem to have appreciated the scenic beauty of the south of France. The rock drawings in the Grotte Cosquer near Cassis, like the cave art of the Grotte Chauvet in the valley of the Ardèche, are among the most impressive surviving artifacts of early human settlement in the region.

Most of these spectacular finds were made by chance, for example in Quinson. Here, during construction work on a reservoir dam on the Verdon, numerous sites of prehistoric settlement were found that would have been lost forever beneath the waters when the valley was flooded. In a rescue campaign at that time, efforts were made to save as many remains of early human history as possible in Haute-Provence.

In order to present the finds in a suitable manner, the decision was made to build a striking new museum, which cost 25 million euros and was opened in 2001. It was designed by the star architect Lord Norman Foster, whose well-known works include the Gherkin, the Millennium Bridge and City Hall in London. For the museum Foster took inspiration from prehistoric caves and the natural course of the river Verdon, putting most of the post-modern building beneath the ground. The construction of a dry-stone wall was also a reference to the local architectural tradition.

This means that visitors are in a sense immersed in the prehistoric world. There are impressive multimedia presentations on geography and the conditions of life for early humans, which changed radically between the Stone Age and the Bronze Age. In addition to finds such as hand axes and flintstones, there is a walk-through reconstruction of a cave and a prehistoric village that was built close to the museum. The guided tours around one of the nearby sites where finds were made, the Grotte de la Baume Bonne, are especially informative.

◀Musée

Address 04500 Quinson, www.museeprehistoire.com | Directions Quinson lies on the D 13 between Riez and Barjols. The museum is 200 metres south of the village, clearly signposted. | Opening times July, Aug. daily 10am–8pm, April–June, Sept Wed–Mon 10am–7pm, Feb, March, Oct–Dec Wed–Mon 10am–6pm | Tip Tours of the Grotte de la Baume Bonne take place in July and August, Wed and Sat at 9.15am, between March and October on the first Sat of the month at 9.15am; book under tel. 0033/0492740959.

87__The Roman Temple

Four columns with a lot of history

Riez is a small, unassuming provincial town on the edge of the Plateau de Valensole, which is known for its lavender fields. At first glance the sleepy village seems little different from others in Haute-Provence, and the only times when it is a scene of bustling activity are Wednesdays and Saturdays – the market days.

However, this appearance is deceptive: in a small park on the banks of the Colostre, the Colonnes Antiques – four six-metre-tall granite columns with Corinthian capitals that bear an architrave – serve as reminders of the important Roman town that once existed here.

The columns are the remains of a podium temple that must have stood in the centre of Roman Riez and have looked similar to those that can be seen in Vienne and Nîmes. Further relics of Roman times, including the foundations of baths and the piers of a bridge, were discovered during excavations. Because the finds are scattered across the plain, historians believe that Roman Riez probably had approximately 20,000 inhabitants.

Colonia Julia Augusta Apollinaris Reiorum (today's Riez) was thus the most important Roman town in Haute-Provence, ahead of those in Sisteron and Digne. The Romanisation of Haute-Provence took place along the Via Domitia – which ran through the valley of the Durance and linked the Rhône plain to Piedmont in northern Italy, and through the influence of the already existing Roman towns of Vaison-la-Romaine, Apt and Carpentras. Riez became the seat of a bishop in late antiquity and retained its status for a long time. In 439 a church council was held here, but in the early Middle Ages the inhabitants abandoned the town and withdrew to higher terrain, which was easier to defend. Roman Riez was forgotten, as a large area of the town was covered up due to flooding by the river Co-lostre.

Address 04500 Riez | **Directions** Riez is close to Lac de Sainte-Croix at the crossing of the D 11 and D 952. The temple stands in a small park on the banks of the Colostre. | **Tip** 100 metres south of the Colonnes Antiques an early Christian baptistery can be seen; it dates from the 6th century and is one of the oldest religious buildings in Provence.

88__The Roundabout

A circular business card

The French love roundabouts. Since a few cars first circulated around the Arc de Triomphe in Paris in 1907, their enthusiasm has known no bounds: with an unbelievable 30,000 ronds-points, France possesses half of all the roundabouts in the world!

For a French driver there is seemingly nothing nicer than to merge skilfully into the flow of traffic on a roundabout and then to leave it again without attracting attention, preferably without using the indicator light.

Especially since 1984, when the controversial rule giving priority to traffic from the right was abandoned, the road builders of the Grande Nation have shown unquestioning devotion to the roundabout, with the intention of easing the traffic flow. This is an understandable project − for a driver with sporting ambitions, what could be worse than standing still at red traffic lights?

In Provence there are roundabouts of every shape and size, from single-lane to multi-lane; the number of exits depends only on the radius, and can easily be increased to as many as eight. Critics point out that this form of traffic regulation takes up more space, but in the European state with the largest surface area, this argument counts for little. As an extra benefit, a roundabout at the entrance to a town considerably reduces the speed of cars.

Sometime before the end of the last century, an inventive landscape architect or tourism manager (perhaps it was an imaginative local politician) seems to have hit on the idea of using the boring islands in the middle of roundabouts for advertising.

Since then hardly a single roundabout at the edge of Provençal towns has been without ancient amphorae, wild bulls or colourful boats. Everywhere, investments are being made in the image of towns. A truly original version is the roundabout with lavender bushes or olive trees …

Directions Approach a roundabout at slightly reduced speed, in readiness to brake. If no other car is in sight, you can skilfully let your own momentum take you through the roundabout. | Tip If the landscaping of the roundabout is more attractive than usual, why not go round a second time?

89 The Ochre Quarries

Where everything shines red

Like glowing wounds, the ochre quarries of Roussillon stand out from the lush green Provençal landscape. Even back in Roman times, the village that sits on an imposing rock of ochre was known as the "vicus russulus" ("red village"). The pigments gained by extracting ochre were used for adorning house façades, but eventually became obsolete in the face of paints manufactured on an industrial scale.

The ochre quarries of Roussillon, which closed down several decades ago, can easily be explored on an educational trail (Sentier des Ocres) that begins at the edge of the village. Two paths, paved in places, lead through the bizarre rock formations of the quarry zone on a walk of 35 to 50 minutes. Here and there the rain has washed the sandstone away to create column shapes. Depending on the degree of oxidisation and its intensification by the play of light and shadows, the spectrum of colours on view ranges from saffron yellow and fiery carmine to an intense wine red and radiant violet.

Thanks to Samuel Beckett the ochre quarries of Roussillon found their way into literary history. From 1942 until the end of the war, Beckett and his partner Suzanne Deschevaux-Dumesnil lived in hiding in Roussillon (he was being sought by the Germans as a member of the resistance in Paris).

Initially they lived in a hotel in the village, later in a small house at its edge, close to the crossing point of the roads to Goult and Apt.

It was a retiree's life. In the evenings Beckett worked on his novel Watt and pondered over his definitive absurd drama Waiting for Godot. In this masterpiece the protagonists Vladimir and Estragon remember a place where they helped to harvest grapes with the words: "Everything glows so red there."

Address 84220 Roussillon | **Directions** Roussillon lies ten kilometres west of Apt on the D 104. Parking spaces and the path to the ochre quarries are well signposted. | **Tip** In a former ochre factory, Usine Mathieu (Conservatoire des Ocres), on the D 104 about 1.5 kilometres to the east, the production of ochre is demonstrated. Visits daily from 9am until 6pm; www.okhra.com.

90__Pont Flavien

A bridge as a status symbol

The Romans, as is well known, were masters of the art of building bridges and roads. Their infrastructure set standards that were unsurpassed during the Middle Ages. It was not until the age of the Enlightenment that other parts of Europe, including France, began to establish a transportation network that could compete with the Romans' in terms of speed of travel.

Nevertheless, some Roman roads and bridges remained in use until quite recently.

Provence possesses so many ancient buildings that an individual Roman bridge attracts little special attention. However, Pont Flavien on the Via Iulia Augusta, which leads from Marseille to Arles and is an extension of the Via Aurelia, is different from other bridges. It was not constructed purely for utility, but is an arch framed by two imposing gates. It spans the little river Touloubre and has a length of more than 25 metres. The donor who lived close by and had it built (the inscription on the bridge names a Roman patrician called Claudius Donnius Flavius) presumably wanted to underline his social status by means of this monument.

The gated arches, which date from the first century AD and are adorned with Corinthian pilasters, bear the lions and eagles typical of the Augustan tradition. The delicate forms of the bridge and its artistic execution have caused art historians to compare it to the famous Maison Carrée in Nîmes.

However, of the four stone lions, two of which stand on each of the cornices of the gates, three are replicas made in the 18th century, and only the one above the southeastern gate pillar is the surviving original.

During the Second World War, when a country road still passed over this bridge, the arches were damaged by trucks, but have since been largely restored.

Address 13250 Saint-Chamas | **Directions** Saint-Chamas is 15 kilometres south of Salon-de-Provence. Flavien stands at the southern edge of the village. | **Tip** Saint-Chamas has a fishing harbour with a long tradition and a Baroque parish church.

91 Pierre Écrite

A mysterious inscription

The Forêt de Fontbelle, which lies to the east of Sisteron, is one of the loveliest forested areas in Haute-Provence. The woods are not easily accessible, as only a few uneven tracks lead up to scattered farms and small villages such as Saint-Geniez. Today there would probably still be no proper road leading up to the mountains, which are more than 2000 metres high, if an ambitious Roman had not tackled this challenge.

The man in question was the Roman prefect Claudius Postumus Dardanus, who built the first road up to Saint-Geniez in the 5th century. The sophistication of its construction (several narrow places had to be negotiated) is evidenced by the fact that the modern département road takes the same route. At the narrowest point, just beyond a small bridge, an inscription in a rock wall commemorates Claudius Postumus Dardanus and gives this passage the name it has to this day, the Canyon of the Inscribed Rock (Défilé de Pierre Écrite).

The inscription not only records that Dardanus caused this road to be built but also that, following his conversion to Christianity and baptism, he and his wife Naevia Galla withdrew to the mountains of Provence with a few followers in order to devote themselves entirely to their religious faith. He is said to have lived in a lonely hermitage named Theopolis, which he fortified with the help of a certain Claudius Lepidus in order to defend himself against the barbarians. Here, in a place of solitude, the Roman prefect planned to put into practice the City of God propagated by Saint Augustine.

It has never been possible to find the exact location of Theopolis, but there is a hypothesis that the late antique foundations that have been excavated between Chardavon and Saint-Geniez might be the remains of this small settlement.

Address 12130 Saint-Geniez | **Directions** From Sisteron the D 3 leads up towards Saint-Geniez, and after eight kilometres to the Pierre Écrite. La Vallée Sauvage is a small animal park in Saint-Geniez with red deer, mouflons and wild boar, open from Easter till October; www.lavalleesauvage.com.

92 __ The Portal of the Abbey Church

A medieval picture book

Saint-Gilles is one of the many stations on the Way of St James and also – thanks to the relics of the hermit Gilles (Aegidius), who lived nearby and is said to have founded the abbey – a place of pilgrimage itself. The flow of pilgrims increased steadily, until the old Romanesque abbey church had to be replaced by a new building. From the previous church, only the spacious crypt, where the bones of Saint Gilles are kept, remains.

The church of the former abbey is famous for the wonderful sculptural decoration on its west façade. This dates from the second half of the 12th century and covers the whole width of the building. The three portals, too, are framed by sculpture. The monumental, eleven-metre-high showpiece façade is reminiscent of the back walls of the stages of Roman theatres, and was the model on which the façade of Saint-Trophime in Arles was based. The iconographic programme derives from the Old and the New Testament. The scenes depicted range from the murder of Abel by Cain to a Majestas Domini in the arch above the middle door. The Passion of Christ, above all, is rendered in great detail as a coherent cycle. Next to it, the raising of Lazarus with Mary and Mary Magdalene is depicted, in order to incorporate the Provençal saints into the programme and to increase their prestige.

Art historians assume that several sculptors worked on the church and believe they can identify three different masters, who previously worked in Toulouse, Burgundy, and northern France, respectively. There seems to have been no shortage of money for the undertaking, as Saint-Gilles was an important commercial centre with approximately 40,000 inhabitants in the high Middle Ages.

During the Wars of Religion the church was seriously damaged, but fortunately the figural decoration on the façade was not lost.

Address Place de l'Église, 30800 Saint-Gilles | Directions Saint-Gilles is 20 kilometres west of Arles and is reached via the N572. | Opening times Sept–June daily 9am–noon and 2–5pm, July, Aug daily 9am–noon and 3–7pm | Tip Diagonally opposite the church is the Maison Romane, the house in which Pope Clement IV was born. Many archaeological finds can be seen here daily from 9am until noon and from 2pm to 5pm.

93__Max Ernst's House

An almost forgotten artist's paradise

The hemmed-in, plain-looking house on the northern edge of Saint-Martin-d'Ardèche would probably not be favoured with a second glance if the façade were not decorated with an oversized, strange-looking relief. Anyone who thinks that the house owner has given free range to his imagination here would not be wrong, but few people would guess that this was the work of the great Surrealist artist Max Ernst.

After cutting free from the Paris Surrealists and separating from his wife, in 1937 Ernst settled in Saint-Martin-d'Ardèche in the south of France with his muse Leonora Carrington, who was then only 20 years old. A year later this oddly matched couple purchased a house, whose walls the artist adorned with a large number of cement reliefs. He placed peculiar-looking creatures, hybrids of humans and animals, on the façade. They give one the impression that they are protecting the home and passionate love of Max and Leonora.

After France's declaration of war on Germany in 1939, Ernst was first interned as an enemy alien, but was soon allowed to return to Leonora in Saint-Martin-d'Ardèche. After a second spell of imprisonment in the infamous camp at Les Milles, with the assistance of a committee led by Varian Fry, he succeeded in escaping to safety abroad, emigrating from Marseille to New York in 1941. In the meantime, Leonora had sold the house and many works of art, and had left France herself.

The works that remained in the house, including many paintings and a series of large cement sculptures, later found their way onto the art market through dubious channels. Today the house has the status of a protected monument and is in private ownership, which means that it, and its "Loplop" relief, can only be viewed from outside.

Address Les Alliberts, 07700 Saint-Martin-d'Ardèche | **Directions** Saint-Martin is at the end of the Gorges de l'Ardèche, 15 kilometres west of the A7, exit to Bollène; there are no signs to the house, but it is easy to find in the Les Alliberts district northeast of the centre. | **Tip** The Office de Tourisme provides an interesting leaflet and a film about Max Ernst.

94__ The Canal de Provence
Provence's waterway

The Canal du Midi is probably the best-known manmade waterway in the south of France, if not in the whole of Europe. Given the status of a World Heritage site by UNESCO, it adorns many coffee-table books and brochures, depicted with plane trees lining its towpaths.

The Canal de Provence, by contrast, despite its resonant name, has never made it onto a book cover. Although it passes through the most beautiful areas of Provence, it is not possible to travel along it in a houseboat, and only parts of its banks are accessible to walkers. It even lacks its own English-language article in Wikipedia.

Built in 1964, the Canal de Provence was not constructed as a means of transport, but to ensure the supply of drinking water to Provence.

Adopting the Roman method – though without the elegance of the Pont du Gard – a channel was constructed that is fed from the upper reaches of the Verdon. At an altitude of 340 metres, up to 40 cubic metres of water per second are taken from the river and sent down to the coast – a distance of 270 kilometres, half of which is a subterranean canal.

In a broad bed of concrete with many branches and side channels, the canal flows through Provence. Reservoirs, pumping stations and treatment facilities help to clean and filter the water before it reaches consumers in the regions of Marseille and Toulon. About two million people in Provence are supplied by this water system, which includes a network of pipes some 4000 kilometres long. In addition, it serves the needs of many agricultural businesses, which could not cultivate their fields without it.

Were it not for the Canal de Provence, the markets of the region would be much less colourful: there would be no melons from Cavaillon, no leeks from Pertuis, and no courgettes from Cucuron.

Address 83116 Saint-Maximin-la-Sainte-Baume | **Directions** Seven kilometres south of Saint-Maximin-la-Sainte-Baume (towards Mazaugues), the small D 64 crosses the Canal de Provence. | **Tip** A further 20 kilometres south of Signes, the Canal de Provence can also be seen.

95 __ The Observatory

Close to heaven

The fact that colours and smells are more intense in Provence is probably something that has been appreciated since Roman times. And not only that: in Haute-Provence the air is clearer than in other parts of France, as so few clouds cover the sky. For this reason, the decision was made in 1937 to build an observatory in the region.

For the site of the observatory, a plateau west of the Durance at a height of 650 metres was chosen, as conditions are ideal there for astronomers on more than 220 nights per year. In fact, 170 nights are completely cloud-free, and the visibility is significantly reduced only when the mistral blows. Research work started in 1943 with a telescope 1.20 metres long. Since then three more telescopes, with lengths of 0.80, 1.52 and 1.93 metres, have been added.

The Observatoire de Haute-Provence is one of the leading centres of astronomical research in the whole of Europe. One spectacular success here was the discovery in 1995 of "51 Pégasi." 50 light years from Earth, it is the first known planet outside our solar system that orbits around a star similar to the sun. In 1998 two further planets, "14 Herculis" and "Gliese 876," were spotted from the observatory. To date, no less than 19 exoplanets have been discovered at the Observatoire de Haute-Provence.

A full staff of scientists from France and abroad work and live all year round in Saint-Michel, which is visible from far away thanks to the 13 domes of the observatory. The universe is investigated here not only by astronomers, but also by geophysicists who, for example, use a laser probe to examine the upper layers of the Earth's atmosphere. The observatory is also accessible to interested laypeople at special visiting times, when it is possible to take a look into the infinite expanses of space through the famous 1.93-metre-long telescope.

Address 04870 Saint-Michel-l'Observatoire, www.obs-hp.fr | **Directions** The Observatoire de Haute-Provence is at the end of the D 305, two kilometres north of Saint-Michel-l'Observatoire. | **Opening times** Tours: July, Aug Tue, Wed, Thu 2, 2.45, 3.30, 4.15 and 5pm, April–June and Sept–early Nov Wed 2.15, 3 and 4pm | **Tip** The village of Saint-Michel, which was built on the foundations of a Celtic oppidum, is also worth visiting.

96__ The Mas de l'Amarine

An overnight stay with modern art in
traditional surroundings

Chambres d'hôtes long ago replaced hotels and campsites as the most popular places to stay in Provence. This is the French version of a bed & breakfast, now a widespread form of accommodation in France that can consist of much more than a few basic guest rooms with boring furnishings. Some of them are rural estates, or even attractive aristocratic townhouses or chateaux where one or several rooms are available for guests to rent. The official regulations limit the number of rooms that can be rented to five with a maximum of 15 guests, and require that the owner live in the same building or an adjacent one.

One of the most beautiful and unusual chambres d'hôtes in Provence is the Mas de l'Amarine, which was opened in 2011 by a young couple with experience in the gastronomic trade. When Alice and Bernard discovered this traditional Provençal farm on the edge of the Alpilles, they fell in love with it at once and knew that they could fulfil their dreams here. The Mas de l'Amarine used to be one of the largest rustic estates in the region. In the 1950s it was purchased by the painter Roger Bezomes, who set up his studio here.

Alice and Bernard were fascinated by this combination of tradition and art when they bought the Mas de l'Amarine. Its interior decoration represents a deliberate break with the usual view of what typical Provençal rooms look like. The dominant colours in the extremely comfortable rooms and suites are red and black. The lobby and the common rooms are enlivened by bright mosaics and sculptures, and paintings by Roger Bezomes can still be seen in the restaurant. In the evening Bernard runs the kitchen, spoiling the guests with cuisine of a very high standard, while Alice looks after the service with great competence. For guests' relaxation, the Mas de l'Amarine has its own pool.

Address 13210 Saint-Rémy-de-Provence, Ancienne voie aurélia, tel. 0033/0490944783, www.mas-amarine.com | **Directions** Saint-Rémy-de-Provence lies between Tarascon and Cavaillon on the D 99. To reach the Mas de l'Amarine, turn left one kilometre south of the village and drive straight on for two more kilometres. | **Tip** The restaurant is open to non-residents.

97 __ A Mausoleum and a Triumphal Arch

Mysterious Roman remains

Provence was one of the first and most important provinces of the Roman Empire. The Romans covered the south of France with a network of roads, bridges and viaducts, and founded cities such as Arles, Orange and Aix-en-Provence, which are among the most impressive in the region. Other Roman cities, for example Glanum to the south of Saint-Rémy, fell into decay in late antiquity and were forgotten.

Until 1921, when excavations began, only two monuments, known as "Les Antiques," served as reminders of the Roman city. Built directly on the road to Maussane-les-Alpilles, the mausoleum, which is freely accessible, and the neighbouring triumphal arch can hardly be overlooked.

To be precise, the triumphal arch is a gate for the foundation of the town. It was built in the reign of Augustus, and is therefore the oldest such gate in Provence. It is adorned by a number of reliefs, which depict olive branches and Gauls bound in chains. As its attic storey is missing, it appears less imposing than the city gate in Orange.

The mausoleum, which is approximately 2000 years old, is of more interest to art historians. The circular temple, decorated with arcades and fluted columns, rises to a height of some 18 metres in several storeys. The monument is crowned by a conical roof. Today it is no longer possible to ascertain exactly whom the mausoleum was dedicated to. Most probably it was not – contrary to many accounts – built for two grandsons of Emperor Augustus who died young, but for the parents of a non-noble family that had attained prestige and wealth in the time of Caesar. Even state-of-the-art genetic investigations would not be capable of answering the question: despite its name, the mausoleum does not contain a grave.

Address 13210 Saint-Rémy-de-Provence | **Directions** Saint-Rémy-de-Provence lies between Tarascon and Cavaillon on the D 99. The Roman monuments are one kilometre to the south on the D 5. | **Tip** The nearby excavation site of Glanum is open daily, April–September, 9.30am–6.30pm, Oct–Feb daily except Mon 10am–5pm.

98 Saint-Paul-de-Mausole
Van Gogh's "lunatic asylum"

When Vincent van Gogh and Provence are mentioned, most people think first of all of Arles, where the eccentric genius came to live in February 1888. His paintings of sunflowers, and the scandals that culminated in van Gogh cutting off his own ear, are now common knowledge amongst those who are interested in art.

What is less well known is that van Gogh lived for more than a year in a privately run psychiatric clinic on the edge of Saint-Rémy. When the citizens of Arles succeeded in having him forcibly committed to an institution, van Gogh submitted to this and decided to move to nearby Saint-Rémy.

The monastery there, situated on the south edge of the town, had been converted into a hospital for the mentally ill in the first half of the 19th century. Here in Saint-Paul-de-Mausole, van Gogh found the peace that he had hoped for. He lived in this "lunatic asylum" surrounded by olive groves for more than a year, until 16 May 1890. During that period he painted some of his most beautiful works, including "Starry Night" and various motifs from the monastery garden.

The outbuildings of the 12th-century monastery are still home to a therapeutic facility for treating the mentally ill. The Romanesque complex with its surviving original church is open to the public.

On the way to the cloister, visitors walk past many faithful reproductions of works that van Gogh painted while he was in Saint-Paul-de-Mausole.

The finest sight here is the cloister with its triple arches, each of which is borne by two pairs of columns. Stairs lead up to a small exhibition about the conditions in the institution during van Gogh's time and a room reconstructed to resemble the one that he occupied.

Address Chemin Saint-Paul, 13210 Saint-Rémy-de-Provence, www.saintpauldemausole.fr | Directions Saint-Rémy-de-Provence lies between Tarascon and Cavaillon on the D 99. The monastery is 1.5 kilometres further south. | Opening times Daily 9.30am–7pm, Nov–March 10.15am–4.45pm | Tip The cloister has capitals with intricately detailed carvings, decorated with intertwined tendrils.

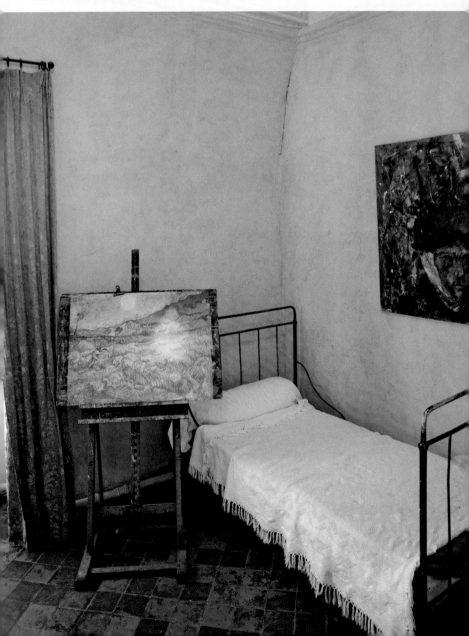

99__ The Transhumance
The shepherds' route

"Transhumance" – the word is spelled the same in French and English – refers to the moving of herds up to their summer pastures and down again to lower slopes when the season ends. In Provence there are no high-altitude mountain pastures, as in the Alps, but here too the word "transhumance" has the same essential meaning, deriving from the Latin "trans" (as in "transit") and "humus" (the ground or earth).

The tradition of transhumance reaches far back into the past. Each May, when the earth would start to suffer from lack of rain and the pastures down in the plains were grazed bare, herds of sheep were taken to the summer pastures by their shepherds, always along the same traditional routes. There is evidence in the archives that about 50,000 sheep were moved every year in the late Middle Ages in Aix-en-Provence.

Like many other rustic customs, the practice of transhumance has almost died out in many parts of Provence. Industrialisation means that animal husbandry is only of marginal importance, and many of the old-established routes have been replaced by the modern road network. However, in 1984 the shepherds of Saint-Rémy-de-Provence decided to revive the old tradition. Since then they have gathered in the town with their herds each year for the "Fête de la Transhumance" on the Monday of Whitsuntide in late morning. In traditional costumes, and with their shepherd's crooks and sheepdogs, they drive the herds of ewes and rams twice around the old quarter of town, watched by a large crowd of spectators. The whole town is filled with the sound of the bleating of more than 4000 animals. In past times the herds were on the road to their summer pastures for about ten days, but nowadays the shepherds of Saint-Rémy take advantage of modern technology and load their sheep into animal transporters.

Address 13210 Saint-Rémy-de-Provence | **Directions** Saint-Rémy-de-Provence lies between Tarascon and Cavaillon on the D 99. | **Tip** The Musée des Alpilles on Place Favier has a lovingly assembled collection on folk traditions.

100__ Watering Holes for Animals

Drinking places hewn out of the rock

The terrain of karst limestone above Saint-Saturnin-lès-Apt is an extremely stony, inhospitable area. In order to keep sheep and cattle there, the farmers had to create artificial watering holes. They cut basins out of the hard rock to collect rainwater. Similar drinking spots for animals can also be found on the Plateau de Sault east of Mont Ventoux, but they are much less numerous there than in the mountains of Saint-Saturnin-lès-Apt, the "Pays des Aiguiers" ("Land of the Drinking Troughs").

These stone basins, usually between one and two metres deep, are known as "aiguiers," which is derived from the Latin word "aquarium." They were made by hand, the result of decades of labour by the farmers and shepherds of the region. To be exact, the aiguiers are only part of a complex system of water supply, as they are fed by several small rock channels and retention basins. To prevent the water from evaporating or being contaminated, a "borie" of dry-stone walls was usually built above the basins.

It is relatively easy to find the aiguiers: in Saint-Saturnin-lès-Apt, first go to the château that lies on an elongated ridge, then climb up further to the chapel situated behind it.

This is the starting point of a trail marked with a horizontal yellow line, which leads to many aiguiers. After only half an hour's walk, you reach the first two watering holes, the Aiguiers Bessons. Later, you come upon the Grand Aiguier de Gayeoux and the Aiguiers de Travignon, with their retention basins and channels in the rock, where the method of collecting water can be observed especially clearly. In a long curve, the route then returns to Saint-Saturnin-lès-Apt, where the effort of undertaking the hike is rewarded with spectacular views of the countryside between Mont Ventoux and the Luberon.

Address 84490 Saint-Saturnin-lès-Apt | Directions Saint-Saturnin-lès-Apt is ten kilometres north of Apt on the D 943. The aiguiers are above the village. | Tip The windmill of Saint-Saturnin-lès-Apt is a typical example of a Provençal mill, as its set-back roof presents a small surface to the mistral.

101 The Salt Works

In the land of white mountains

Salt has always been a popular substance for conserving food, and in the age of industrialisation the demand for it increased significantly. In order to meet the rising need for salt in the soap factories in Marseille, a salt works was opened in the east of the Camargue in 1856. Within a few decades it became the largest in Europe.

In those years the workers' town of Salin-de-Giraud was founded with a chequerboard grid layout. With its little grey houses and front gardens that unfortunately lack the loveliness of the Midi, Salin is a little bit reminiscent of the sad-looking miners' towns of northern France.

Today the salt works cover an area of 11,000 hectares. The annual output amounts to more than 800,000 tons of sea salt! In order to produce it, Mediterranean seawater, which normally contains about 3.6 grams of salt per litre, has to be channelled through several evaporation basins. As this happens, it is saturated with chlorine and sodium so that the salt content rises to 260 grams per litre. The sea salt can then be "harvested" using implements that look like rakes.

At harvest time, which usually lasts from the end of August until October, the heaps of salt – they are called camelles – resemble a barren winter landscape.

From a viewing platform ("point de vue sur les salines") visitors have a fantastic panoramic view of the extensive salt works and storage facilities.

The salt that is made in Salin-de-Giraud is used in the chemical industry for the most part; table salt, by contrast, is harvested nearby in Aigues-Mortes (Salins du Midi).

The finest salt with the most intense taste finds its way to the shops under the name "fleur de sel"; this "salt flower" can only be harvested on hot, windless days by removing an extremely thin layer of salt using a wooden shovel.

Address 13129 Salin-de-Giraud | Directions The salt works are three kilometres south of Salin-de-Giraud, which in turn lies 35 kilometres south of Arles on the D36. | Tip A small boutique at the car park sells various local products, including fleur de sel, of course.

102 The Jean Moulin Monumen

France's greatest resistance fighter

To this day Jean Moulin is revered in France as the greatest hero of the résistance. Hundreds of streets and schools are named after him, and in 1993 a two-franc coin bearing his likeness was issued. In Provence he is honoured in the form of a monument, as on the night of 1 January 1942 he and two companions parachuted to earth in the Alpilles north of Salon-de-Provence in order to coordinate the work of different resistance groups, a commission he received from Charles de Gaulle.

The bronze sculpture by Marcel Courbier depicts a larger-than-life-sized figure, stretching its arms to the sky.

Jean Moulin, who was born in 1899 in Béziers in the south of France, supported the resistance movement early in the war when he was still a prefect in regional government. He put his life at risk by returning to France from London to establish, after long negotiations with various resistance groups, the Conseil National de la Résistance (CNR), which considerably improved the effectiveness of the movement. Politically the CNR was close to the programmes of the socialists and communists.

Moulin, living in the underground, was the first name on German lists of wanted persons. Feverish activities were carried out all over France to search for him. On 21 June 1943 he fell into the hands of the Nazis in Caluire near Lyon and was subject to terrible torture, but did not reveal anything about his contacts. A few weeks later, after further brutal mistreatment, Moulin died on a train that was taking him to Germany.

The significance of his work for the success of the French résistance is undisputed. He received a major posthumous honour: at the behest of President de Gaulle in 1964, his mortal remains were transported to the Panthéon, the national temple to great French figures in Paris.

Address 13300 Salon-de-Provence, www.memorialjeanmoulin.fr | Directions Four kilometres north of Salon-de-Provence, on N 538 towards Cavaillon | Tip In memory of Jean Moulin the roads between Salon-de-Provence, Eygalières and Saint-Andiol were named "Chemin de la Liberté."

103__ The Seer
A man with a solution to every problem

Salon-de-Provence is associated with the name of Nostradamus. This famous prophet was born under the name Michel de Nostredame in nearby Saint-Rémy-de-Provence and studied in Marseille and Montpellier, but Salon-de-Provence is the place where he is almost ubiquitous. In addition to a modern monument in the town, the façade of a whole building is covered with a giant-sized portrait of him. This colourful mural is controversial, as it looks a little bit like the work of an anonymous Provençal graffiti artist with a tendency towards kitsch.

All over the world Nostradamus is revered for his dark and mystic prophecies. His followers have no doubt about the truth of his predictions, while his critics regard him as a dubious charlatan and claim that the figments of his imagination, which are wreathed in scarcely decipherable anagrams and newly-coined words, are so general that they cannot stand up to detailed examination. In esoteric circles the matter is viewed differently, of course.

Salon-de-Provence is well aware of the drawing-power of its most famous resident and is skilled at attracting visitors to the "Maison de Nostradamus." However, it is difficult to leave the thoroughly renovated house in which Nostradamus spent the last 19 years of his life with his second wife and six children, and from where he published his famous prophecies, without a feeling of disappointment. The Maison provides very little information and has more the character of a waxworks museum, where the colourful figures and scenes do more to discredit the Nostradamus myth than to shed light on it. There is unfortunately no attempt to conduct a critical examination of the man and his work.

A more worthwhile activity is to walk to the collegiate church of Saint-Laurent on the edge of town, where Nostradamus was buried in 1566.

Address 13300 Salon-de-Provence | Directions Salon-de-Provence is on the A 54 between Arles and Aix-en-Provence. | Opening times Maison de Nostradamus: 11, Rue Nostradamus, daily 9am–noon and 2–6pm, Sat, Sun 2–6pm | Tip At the château there is a garden with healing herbs that Nostradamus is claimed to have used. Campers can spend a night on a campsite named after the prophet; www.camping-nostradamus.com.

104 __ The Memorial Plaque
A forgotten city of literature

Sanary-sur-Mer is sleepy little port with a palm-fringed promenade, pastel-coloured houses and a few lovely sandy beaches. A truly idyllic place for a holiday. Only an inconspicuous memorial plaque on the Office de Tourisme serves as a reminder that Sanary-sur-Mer was once the centre of German literary exiles.

Between 1933 and 1940 there was hardly a single significant German author who did not stay in Sanary at least for a time. Thomas and Golo Mann, Franz Werfel, Ernst Toller, Arnold Zweig, René Schickele, Franz Hessel and Ludwig Marcuse were among the writers who fled from Germany after the seizure of power by the National Socialists in 1933. Some of them, like Lion Feuchtwanger, whose books were more widely read than those of any other German-language author of the 1930s, soon felt at home on the French Mediterranean coast. Feuchtwanger lived in Sanary with his wife Marta and during his time there wrote the major novels The Oppermanns and Exile. The two houses that he occupied, Villa Lazar and Villa Valmer, can still be seen today, though not from inside.

"One walks on the beach; one talks about people, books, problems, about work," was how Klaus Mann described everyday life on the Riviera. It was not long, however, before dark clouds appeared in the exiles' sunny skies: in Provence, as in other parts of France, men born in Germany or Austria had to report to the authorities after the outbreak of war. Although the displaced writers who lived there were opponents of the Nazis, Germans were no longer welcome. The little literary capital on the Mediterranean coast was now ridiculed with the nickname "Sanary-la-Boche." After the end of the war, this aspect of the town's history was neglected for many years. Not until 1987 was the plaque unveiled in memory of the exiled authors.

Address 1, Quai du Levant, 83110 Sanary-sur-Mer | Directions Sanary-sur-Mer lies on the coastal road (D 559) between Bandol and Toulon, about 20 kilometres west of Toulon. The Office de Tourisme is by the harbour. | Tip The Office de Tourisme sells a small book costing three euros about the exiled writers, showing exactly where they lived.

À LA MÉMOIRE DES ÉCRIVAINS ALLEMANDS ET AUTRICHIENS AINSI QU'À LEURS FAMILLES ET AMIS QUI FUYANT LE RÉGIME NATIONAL-SOCIALISTE, SE SONT RETROUVÉS À SANARY-SUR-MER

BERT BRECHT
FERDINAND BRUCKNER
FRITZ BRÜGEL
FRANZ TH.CSOKOR
ALBERT DRACH
LION FEUCHTWANGER
BRUNO FRANK
EMIL J. GUMBEL
WALTER HASENCLEVER
WILHELM HERZOG
FRANZ HESSEL
ALFRED KANTOROWICZ
HERMANN KESTEN
EGEN ERWIN KISCH
ARTHUR KOESTLER
ANNETTE KOLB
MECHTHILDE LICHNOWSKI
ERIKA MANN

GOLO MANN
HEINRICH MANN
KLAUS MANN
THOMAS MANN
VALERIU MARCU
LUDWIG MARCUSE
JULIUS MEIER-GRAEFE
ALFRED NEUMANN
BALDER OLDEN
ERWIN PISCATOR
EMIL ALPHONS REINHARDT
JOSEPH ROTH
FRANZ WERFEL
KURT WOLFF
THEODOR WOLFF
OTTO ZOFF
ARNOLD ZWEIG
STEFAN ZWEIG

DEN DEUTSCHEN UND ÖSTERREICHISCHEN SCHRIFTSTELLERN MIT IHREN ANGEHÖRIGEN UND FREUNDEN, DIE AUF DER FLUCHT VOR DER NATIONALSOZIALISTISCHEN GEWALTHERRSCHAFT IN SANARY-SUR-MER ZUSAMMENTRAFEN

105__ The Insect Paradise
The harmas of Jean-Henri Fabre

Today the name Jean-Henri Fabre is only recognised by a few bio-
logists, although Fabre was one of the leading European insect re-
searchers and among the greatest French scholars.

Fabre is revered as much for his poetic descriptions of the world
of insects as for his pioneering studies about the breeding behaviour
of wasps. At the age of 57 he acquired a small, run-down country estate at the foot of Mont Ventoux in order to be near his beloved insects.

The "Homer of insects" was not only a great researcher but also
a great eccentric. Fabre lived a secluded life in his harmas (the Provençal word for fallow land) as if wrapped in a cocoon, and built a
stone wall around his property.

His contacts were limited to a few inhabitants of the village. If he
ever left his land, it was only for a zoological excursion to the slopes
of Mont Ventoux. He ascended to its striking peak more than
30 times.

His two-storey house with its pink façade and pale green window shutters – now an outstation of the Natural History Museum in
Paris – still lies outside the village. It seems unwelcoming and a little aloof; it is screened by plane, chestnut and fig trees, and by a wall
as tall as a man near the road.

Fabre's study, a large, bright room with two windows that look
out onto the garden, is less the den of a poet than a kind of cabinet
of natural exhibits.

Fabre's floppy hat, his collector's bag and his walking stick are
preserved like religious relics. Behind the house lies the sequestered
garden of the harmas; it is no longer barren fallow land with dry thistles and a few herbs, but an overgrown miniature habitat for Provençal flora and fauna, with shady oaks and cypresses, as well as
countless insects.

Address Route d'Orange, 84830 Sérignan-du-Comtat, www.mnhn.fr/mnhn/harmas-fabre | Directions Sérignan-du-Comtat is on the D976, eight kilometres northeast of Orange. The harmas is well signposted, and lies on the road to Orange, 500 metres outside the village. | Opening times April–June, Sept, Oct Mon, Tue, Thu, Fri 10am–12.30pm and 2.30–6pm, Sat and Sun 3.30–6pm, July, Aug 10am–12.30pm, 1.30–7pm | Tip In the middle of the village is a monument to Jean-Henri Fabre.

106__ The Waterfall
Tropical dreams

The landscape of Provence is associated with lavender, dry garrigue shrubs and gnarled olive trees. In summer the ground is dried out, as water is not plentiful despite the Rhône and Durance. The arable fields groan in the heat and tourists enjoy themselves on the beaches.

With this in mind, those who go walking in the Haut-Var region south of the Grand Canyon du Verdon, will hardly believe their eyes when all of a sudden they come across an enormous, emerald-green waterfall: in a broad curtain of water, the little river Bresque pours from a height of more than 40 metres into a deep, turquoise-coloured pool that seems to have been designed for cooling off.

Nearby Sillans-la-Cascade owes its name to the waterfall, which is regarded as the most beautiful in Provence. This quiet village once belonged to the counts of Castellane, who built a castle here. Sillans with its paved alleys is still largely surrounded by its defensive walls and their round towers, which underlines the fortified look of the village.

From the car park by the château, a 15-minute walk along a marked walking trail leads to the waterfall. The last few metres are the most spectacular part of the walk. Here the vegetation becomes denser, and the scenery looks like a little jungle with large fronds of ferns. The water is crystal clear and fairly cool, as it comes straight from the mountains.

To protect the natural surroundings, for the last few years bathing has unfortunately been prohibited in this wonderful pool. Since many visitors originally ignored the ban, direct access was subsequently barred by means of a wooden fence. The official reason given for this is the danger of falling rocks. As an alternative, visitors have a fine panoramic view from the high ground opposite the waterfall.

Address 83690 Sillans-la-Cascade | Directions Sillans-la-Cascade is between Cotignac and Aups on the D22. | Tip In Sillans there is a single hotel with a restaurant: Les Pins, www.restaurant-lespins.com.

107_ The Rotunda

The village crowned by a mysterious building

Simiane-la-Rotonde is undoubtedly one of the most attractive villages in Provence. Its houses are stacked up the hill like organ pipes. "Villages perchés" of this kind, which have the appearance of an eagle's nest, are typical of Haute-Provence. Simiane, however, stands out not only for its extensive fields of lavender, but above all for its mysterious rotunda, which has even been incorporated into the name of the village.

Due to its unusual shape, for many years the rotunda was thought to be a religious building or a tomb, but it was proven long ago that it was a residential tower, built in the 12th century by the powerful lords of Simiane.

This makes the 18-metre-high donjon the oldest of the towers that were built in the south of France based on examples from the north.

From outside, the massive rotunda, which marks the northwest part of the castle, resembles the misshapen stump of a pyramid. This makes the appearance of its interior all the more surprising. During a restoration a few years ago, a ceiling was re-inserted, and the building now has two storeys again.

The dimly lit, twelve-sided chamber on the upper floor, with its arches, its ribbed vault and its columns decorated with capitals and weathered masks, looks like a castle chapel. At the top of the vaulting is a circular bull's eye. The comparatively low-ceilinged ground floor, which was once thought to have been a tomb chamber, was probably used in past times as a storehouse for provisions or weapons, while on the upper floor, which was entered from the courtyard, receptions or meetings could be held in surroundings that made a good impression.

In case of armed conflict, the rotunda, which once had battlements on its roof, served as a place of refuge.

Address Place du Château, 04150 Simiane-la-Rotonde | Directions Simiane-la-Rotonde lies on the D 51, which links Apt to Banon. The clearly signposted rotunda is situated above the village. | Opening times May–Aug daily 10.30am–1pm and 1.30–7pm, March, April, Sept, Oct Wed–Mon 1–5.30pm | Tip From a small covered public space in the village there is a wonderful view across the valley.

108 The Durance Gap
The gateway to Provence

Sisteron is regarded as the "gateway to Provence." The town is both on the geographical border to Dauphiné and on a culinary border, at the "Frontière du Beurre" and the "Frontière de l'Huile," as butter is traditionally used for cooking north of Sisteron, and olive oil to the south of the town.

Sisteron owes its importance to the river Durance, which comes from the French Alps and carved out its riverbed by breaking through a great rocky massif many, many millions of years ago. The rugged, almost vertical strata of stone of the Rocher de la Baume, falling steeply to the left bank of the river, are highly impressive. Only this narrow gap through which the Durance flows made it possible to open up the northeast of Provence with transport links.

The gap has therefore always been seen as a strategically important place of passage.

The Romans built a fort called "Segustero" here, but hardly any traces of it have remained, apart from a mausoleum that was excavated. The fort and a small settlement around it had the task of securing the Via Domitia, an important military and commercial road that connected France with Italy. Whoever possessed Sisteron also controlled the approach to Provence. This fact was recognised by the powerful counts of Forcalquier, who built the castle high above the town in the Middle Ages.

After severe damage to this fortification in the Wars of Religion, the French monarchy restored the citadel and extended it according to contemporary standards of military engineering with scarped walls and bastions as outworks. At times the citadel was used as a prison – John Casimir, later king of Poland, was once incarcerated behind its thick walls.

At a later date, Napoleon, who took this route on his return to France from Elba, feared that his adventure might end in Sisteron.

Address 04200 Sisteron | Directions Sisteron lies on the A51, which connects Aix-en-Provence with Grenoble. | Tip The citadel and Musée de la Citadelle are open daily from April until mid-November from 9am to 6pm, in the main season until 7pm.

109__ The Castle
A crenellated border fort

Les Baux, Cassis and Mornas – in Provence there are many strong castles, impressive testimony to a warlike era when the region was still independent and surrounded by enemies. One of the most imposing fortifications is the Château de Tarascon, which secured the border to the territories of the powerful kings of France, and was built within sight of Beaucaire.

Construction of the castle began around the year 1400, but was completed only in the reign of René, the last king of Provence, in 1449.

Despite its late date, in many ways the Château de Tarascon embodies the ideal vision of a medieval castle. Inside, however, Renaissance influence is perceptible. Crenellated and protected by a wide moat, the Château de Tarascon stands almost 50 metres above the river Rhône. The main part of the castle, originally entered across a drawbridge, is only accessible via a connecting courtyard; this main building with its rooms for living and for public occasions surrounds another small courtyard.

When Provence became part of France, Tarascon lost its strategic importance, and the castle was used as a prison for a long time. The last prisoners remained until 1926, and shortly afterwards the French state initiated a comprehensive restoration.

Today the only reminders of the castle's use as a prison are some graffiti marks, which have even been recognised as relics with historical value.

A tour of the castle leads visitors through bare, unfurnished rooms. In the dining room and the banqueting hall a few modern wall hangings add some visual interest, and the audience chamber possesses an attractive cross-ribbed vault. Spiral stairs lead up to the roof terrace and a magnificent view across the valley of the Rhône and over to Beaucaire and the Montagnette range.

Address Route de Vallabregues, 13150 Tarascon | Directions Tarascon is situated between Avignon and Arles on the left bank of the Rhône. The château stands right by the river. | Opening times June–Sept daily 9am–6.30pm, Oct–May Tue–Sun 9.30am–5pm | Tip The collegiate church of Sainte-Marthe opposite the château has an impressive crypt with a sarcophagus dating from the 3rd century.

110_ The Baptistery
A chapel in an idyllic village

To call Venasque a village to dream about would be no exaggeration. It spreads over a steep mountain outcrop, and its dry-stone defensive wall with round towers truly seems to be growing out of the bedrock. And Mont Ventoux sends greetings from the distance. Cobblestoned alleys, splashing fountains and small outdoor spaces complete the idyll. Two restaurants and a little village store – that's all there is to Venasque, which belongs to the elite group of "Les Plus Beaux Villages de France" ("The Most Beautiful Villages in France"). The drive over the Col de Murs alone is a pleasure.

The easily defensible heights on which Venasque stands were already settled in Celtic times, and the Romans built a sanctuary here. In the early Middle Ages the bishops of Carpentras took up residence, and thus Venasque was not only an episcopal seat but for almost 500 years served as the "capital" of the Comtat (County) Venaissin.

The foundations of the church of Notre-Dame de Vie, which was built at the highest point in the village, date from late antiquity. As this church is the successor to a cathedral from the period of late antiquity, it was long thought that the baptistery belonging to it might have an origin as early as the 6th century.

However, it is now believed that the baptistery, which was once connected with Notre-Dame de Vie by a passageway, is much more recent. The chapel was probably not originally even used for baptism, but was erected at the turn of the 10th to the 11th century as a chapel dedicated to martyrs or as a funeral chapel, and was converted into a baptistery through the addition of a font only at a later date.

Nevertheless, the "baptistery" with its ground plan in the shape of a Greek cross is still among the oldest religious buildings in Provence.

Address Place de l'Église, 84210 Venasque | Directions Venasque is eleven kilometres south of Carpentras on the D 4. The baptistery stands in the middle of the village. | Opening times April–Oct daily 9am–noon and 1–6.30pm, Nov–March 9.15am–noon and 1–5pm | Tip To stay or dine directly above the city wall, book at the Hotel-Restaurant Les Remparts, www.hotellesremparts.com.

111__The Abandoned Mountain Village

Dreaming of life in Provence

Many people who go to Provence on vacation, dream of living in the sunny south, but very few of them are brave enough to make this fantasy a reality. Annick and Charles Speth, a Belgian couple, thought for a long time about whether they should dare to move there with their three school-age children. When they discovered the ruins of the abandoned Vieil Aiglun in 2002, the decision was made: from that time onwards they turned their backs on cloudy, rainy Belgium and delighted in the Provençal sunshine.

Vieil Aiglun, which lies at a height of 775 metres, shared the fate of many mountain villages in the south of France. An increasing number of inhabitants moved down to the more easily accessible valley, so that Vieil Aiglun became a visibly dilapidated ghost village in the early 20th century. The last residents left in 1942 – since then Vieil Aiglun fell into decay, apart from the fact that the society "Les Amis du Vieil Aiglun" did exemplary work in looking after the late Romanesque church.

Annick and Charles Speth thus bought a scene of ruins and brought it back to life by means of painstaking work. Roofs and walls were lovingly repaired and the whole ensemble of buildings, including a vaulted room with an open fireplace, were restored. At the beginning they rented out five rooms to guests, but later decided to divide the buildings into three well-equipped holiday homes.

Their guests want for nothing: on the extensive premises they find a wonderful pool with a panoramic view, a space for playing boule, table-tennis, a children's playground and several shady places to sit. The view of the summits of Haute-Provence and the southern Alps is stunning. Horses whinny, and if you lie in one of the hammocks and indulge in daydreams, then it feels as if paradise is close at hand.

Address Vieil Aiglun, 04510 Aiglun, www.vieil-aiglun.com | Directions Eight kilometres west of Digne the small D 417 branches off right from the RN 85, and leads three kilometres to Vieil Aiglun, the last part in steep hairpin bends. | Tip Every Thursday from 3.30pm until 7pm the biggest organic market in the département is held in Aiglun.

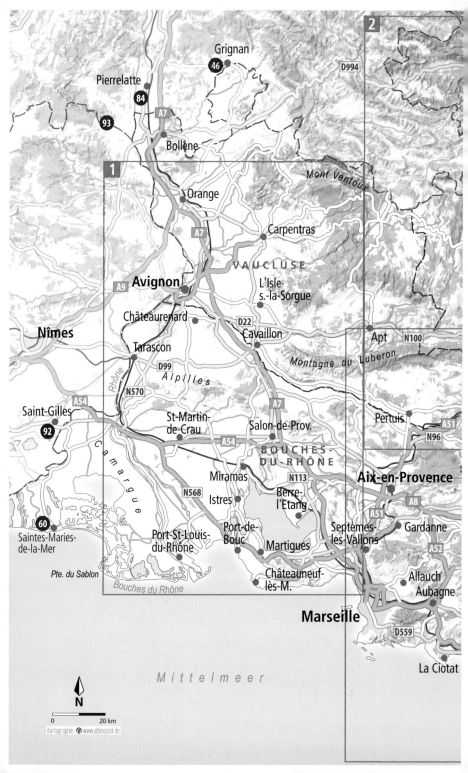

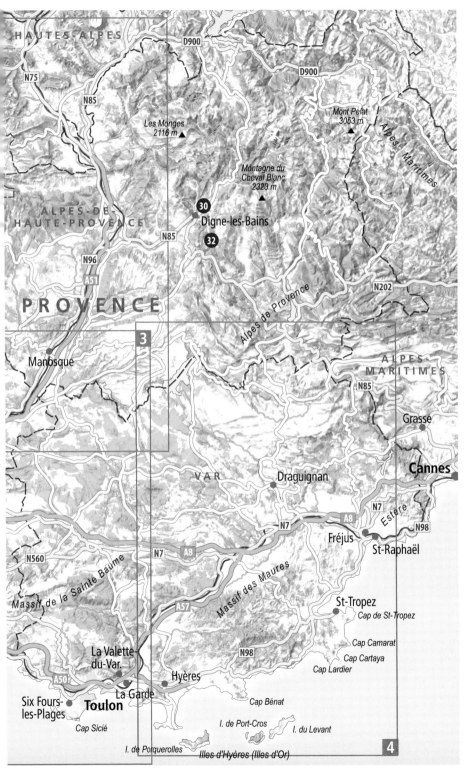

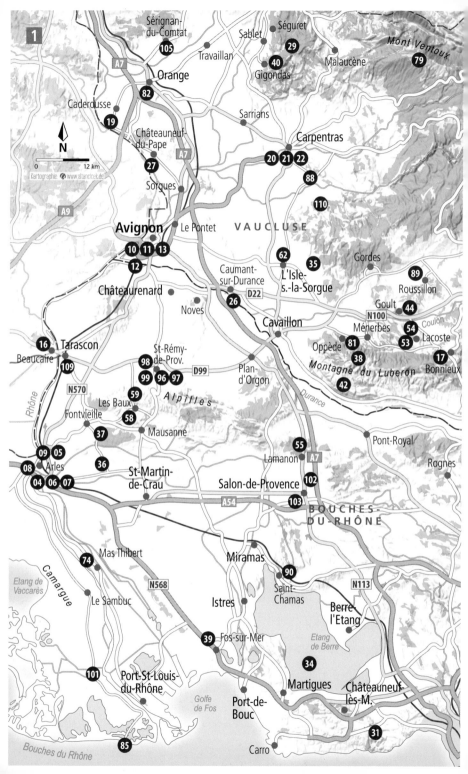

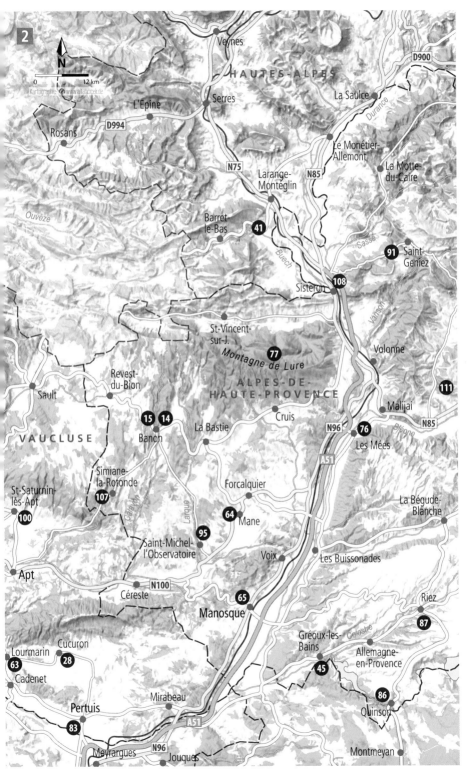

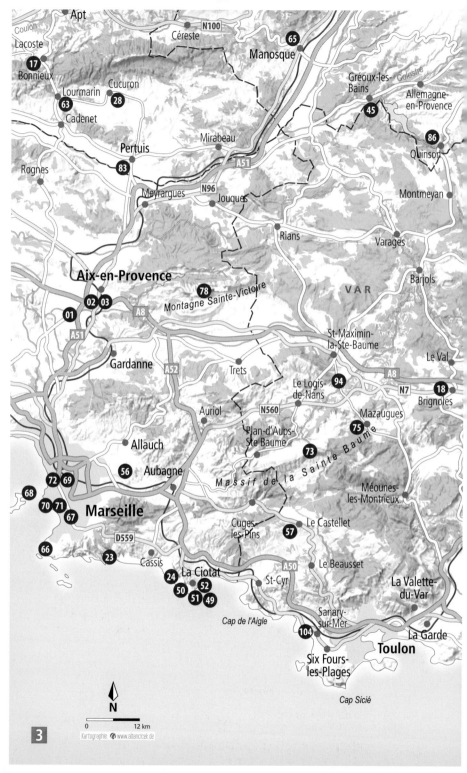

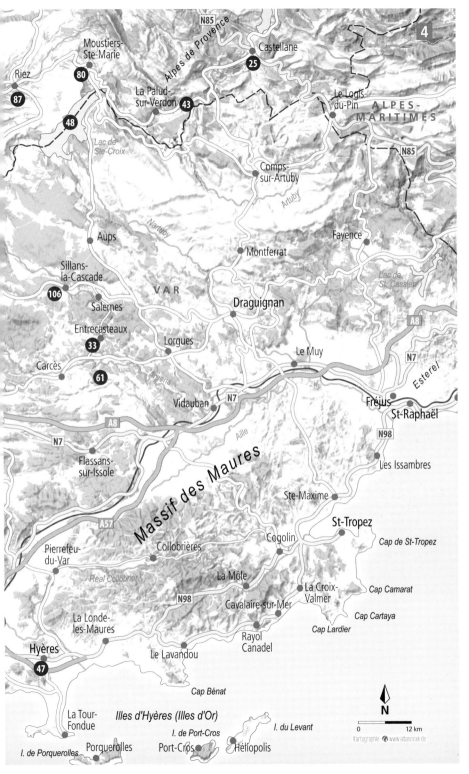

Lucia Jay von Seldeneck,
Carolin Huder, Verena Eidel
**111 PLACES IN BERLIN
THAT YOU SHOULDN'T MISS**
ISBN 978-3-95451-208-9

John Sykes
**111 PLACES IN LONDON
THAT YOU SHOULDN'T MISS**
ISBN 978-3-95451-346-8

Rike Wolf
**111 PLACES IN HAMBURG
THAT YOU SHOULDN'T MISS**
ISBN 978-3-95451-234-8

Paul Kohl
**111 PLACES IN BERLIN
ON THE TRAIL OF THE NAZIS**
ISBN 978-3-95451-323-9

Rüdiger Liedtke
**111 PLACES IN MUNICH
THAT YOU SHOULDN'T MISS**
ISBN 978-3-95451-222-5

Dirk Engelhardt
**111 PLACES IN BARCELONA
THAT YOU MUST NOT MISS**
ISBN 978-3-95451-353-6

Peter Eickhoff
**111 PLACES IN VIENNA
THAT YOU SHOULDN'T MISS**
ISBN 978-3-95451-206-5

Marcus X. Schmid
**111 PLACES IN ISTANBUL
THAT YOU MUST NOT MISS**
ISBN 978-3-95451-423-6

Stefan Spath
**111 PLACES IN SALZBURG
THAT YOU SHOULDN'T MISS**
ISBN 978-3-95451-230-0

Christiane Bröcker,
Babette Schröder
**111 PLACES IN STOCKHOLM
THAT YOU MUST NOT MISS**
ISBN 978-3-95451-459-5

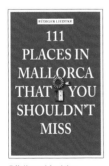

Rüdiger Liedtke
**111 PLACES ON MALLORCA
THAT YOU SHOULDN'T MISS**
ISBN 978-3-95451-281-2

Thanks to Atout France, the Comité Régional de Tourisme Provence-Alpes-Côte d'Azur and the tourist offices of the départements for their help and support, especially Susanne Zurn-Seiler, Ralph Schetter, Monika Fritsch, Michel Caraïsco, Valérie Gillet and Francine Riou. A special thank you goes to Monika Ettl.

The author

Ralf Nestmeyer is a travel journalist and author of several guidebooks to Provence and the south of France. He has also written a book about French poets and their houses, and a literary travel guide to Provence and the Côte d'Azur (Klett-Cotta Verlag). www.nestmeyer.de.